I0622556

locomotive lullaby

riding the grief train
across america and back

by

CHERYL DELLASEGA, PHD

Legacy Book Press
Camanche, Iowa

Copyright © 2023 Cheryl Ann Dellasega

Cover design by Kaitlea Toohey (kaitleatoohey.com)
Cover photography by Cheryl Dellasega

In certain instances, names and identifying characteristics for entities and individuals
have been changed. As it is with all personal narratives, this one is subjective. This
story is told from the author's perspective and her memories; she recognizes that
everyone remembers events differently.

All rights reserved. No part of this book may be used or reproduced by any means,
graphic, electronic, or mechanical, including photocopying, recording, taping or by
any information storage retrieval system without the written permission of the pub-
lisher except in the case of brief quotations embodied in critical articles and reviews.

ISBN: 979-8-9874823-2-2
Library of Congress Case Number: 1-12113754999

Dedicated to, of course, Paul.

table of contents

prologue

The red "Emergency Stop" lever was within easy reach. It was a federal offense to pull it for anything less than an all-out catastrophe, but that's exactly what my life felt like. I had made a terrible mistake and needed to get off the train before I melted down completely.

Take a nice deep breath, the professor voice inside my head said.

My students loved it when I put on soothing music and led them through relaxation exercises, claiming that just a few minutes of concentration in a peaceful place helped reduce their stress. This, like many of the things I taught, was easy to do in a classroom and more difficult to apply in real life.

Breathing out slowly, I focused on the rows of passengers settling into their seats before me, opening laptops or books in preparation for our departure. Clearly, the only person whose heart was pounding in anticipation of a looming crisis was mine.

The train jerked forward, my signal to drop into the closest available seat. For a moment, my wheeled suitcase stayed clenched between my knees, and my backpack, filled to capacity, sat on my lap like my children did in their younger years.

What had I done? Wasn't it enough that in the last twelve months my husband died in an accident, my daughter was kidnapped and sent to prison, and my heart was shredded by my first romance as a widow? These were things that should be treated with a lot of sedation and full retreat to a dark bedroom with my dog, Lacey, and a door that locked out the world. Instead, I came up with a plan that involved living intimately with total strangers while chugging across the country and back again.

For some reason, spending the equivalent of a month's salary to take a train trip from my home state of Pennsylvania to California seemed like a great idea until it actually came time to leave. The items on my travel "to do" list were checked off: 1) Take

Lacey to the kennel, 2) Spend extra time with my three-year-old granddaughter in preparation for the separation, 3) Notify my workplace that I would be out of the office for two weeks, 4) Put my mail on hold, and 5) Warn my family that I might be without cell phone reception at times.

In the last year, lists kept me going. When traumas kept exploding in my life like a chain of chemical reactions, I numbered mundane activities on my calendar each morning and then struck them off with a highlighter (yellow for work, pink for personal, and blue for everything else) at the end of the day. One of my colleagues noted that I was a "striker not a crosser," which she said was supposed to reveal something about my organizational skills.

It didn't matter what technique I used, those lists, even the awful ones—1) Call my daughter's lawyer and see if he can get her out of jail, 2) Sort tax info and take to accountant, 3) Refill meds, 4) Make appointment with GI specialist, and 5) Buy cemetery plot—gave me a sense of purpose. If I could edit a student paper, talk to my daughter's case manager on the phone, email a colleague, return books to the library, call my parents to see how they were doing, and get Lacey groomed, it wouldn't matter if mail from the IRS about our unpaid taxes made it impossible to close my mailbox. A completed to-do list made me feel productive and purposeful, justifying an early retreat to bed and the pills that helped me sleep.

That's why everything was packed and prepared for my trip but me. While waiting on the platform, it was the unwritten concerns that haunted me. How would I have enough energy to stay awake and interact with people for most of the day? Who would I tell the story of Paul's death to in a search for understanding? What need to escape was leading me to board a westbound train headed away from my comfort zone in the Northeast Corridor?

Slumped in my seat, I felt like damaged goods, unable to stop thinking about my husband's last words ("I'll be fine"), the crumpled look on my youngest son's face when he saw his father pronounced dead, or my daughter's screams when she learned what had happened. Did part of me still believe what I taught my students: grief runs its course in a year? Or was I actually following the advice I gave patients on changing behavior: studies show a dramatic change can help jump start a new life?

Tum-tum-tum. The wheels hit the track with a sound like the slow beat of a drum and the car wobbled forward. As we gathered momentum, there was the long ominous churn of metal hitting metal, and the sound of people faded as the noise of machines took over: squeaking, creaking, and rattling. If it had been my first trip, I might have worried that the train was going to shake itself apart, but I was a seasoned traveler and knew that the Amtrak equivalent of turbulence was as much a part of the trip as the scenery spooling by beyond smudged windows.

From the behind me, I heard the conductor call out, "Tickets please, have your tickets ready."

I pulled out my packet of tickets and tried to decide which one should be handed over first. There was no more time for second thoughts —now—I was *"en route,"* once more speeding, completely unprepared, into unknown territory.

before the beginning
june 9, 2009
6:23 a.m.

On our honeymoon, my husband, Paul, suggested that we should establish a routine of kissing each other three times every night before going to sleep. He was half serious, but we gave it a try until a colicky baby came along and required attention 24/7. By the time that colicky baby was grown, Paul was going to bed early and I was staying up late, making those kisses just a memory.

Then came the morning of our final kiss, which was my desperate attempt to keep him alive. Had I ever pressed my lips against his so passionately?

"Come on, honey." Both my body and voice were trembling as I shook his shoulders. "Paul, wake up."

Nothing. The phone was somehow in my hand; had I dashed upstairs to get it, or did I carry it downstairs with me, suspecting problems after hearing a strange sound in our basement? I punched in the numbers and a 911 operator answered instantly.

"What's your emergency?" The male voice was fast, like an experienced deejay.

"It's my husband. He fell on our basement steps and isn't breathing. Please hurry." I didn't want to cry because then I would lose all control, but my words came out as a sob anyway.

"Can I have your name and address?"

We quickly sorted out the details of where I lived and what had happened, and then I was instructed to open the front door and lock up any pets who might interfere with the ambulance crew. In another circumstance, the idea of Lacey, our little Westie, attacking the paramedics in the same way she went after the vacuum cleaner would have been funny, but my focus was Paul, whose lips were the color of blueberries, even when I gave him my own breath.

"I can't go upstairs. I can't leave him." Air in, air out. "Every time I stop, he doesn't breathe on his own, and his lips are cyanotic."

"Is his heart beating?"

It was, which was strange since oxygen deprivation often leads to cardiac arrest, but Paul had a good heart. At night, when I wrapped my left foot around his leg, I would feel his pulse, strong and steady.

I put my ear to my husband's chest again just to be sure and heard the familiar lub-dub. "Yes, his heart seems fine."

"Okay, help is on the way. Take a break and go upstairs and open the door," the operator said.

What a relief. Paul would be taken to the academic medical center where I worked, and the best specialists in the area would give him the right medicines and therapies. He would wake up and come back home, and later, we would laugh nervously about what a klutz he was.

I dashed upstairs and opened the door, checking for the sound of sirens. It was quiet; people in our neighborhood were probably just beginning to wake up.

Back down in the basement, I wasn't quite as upbeat. I had seen patients die slowly and quickly before, touched dead bodies, and even been with people I loved shortly before they died, so I knew what death looked like, so I knew Paul was gone. I knew it before checking all the reflexes that indicate an intact neurological system and got no response.

"Paul, please come back. Don't leave," I said in between deep gulps of oxygen that I forced into his lungs. Comatose people can still hear; maybe my coaxing would bring him back. How many stories had I shared with my students about near death experiences where that exact thing occurred?

My mind was skipping from thought to thought, trying to figure out what had happened so I could offer the ambulance crew helpful diagnostic information. Paul was too smart to trip on steps he went up and down at least once every day, and even if a lapse had made him fall, what would cause him to stop breathing so quickly and completely? Bleeds into the brain are fast, but not that fast.

In the days after his death, I would continue to ask those questions and replay the events of the hour before and after his death, as if they held answers critical to my closure. I would tell anyone who would listen the details over and over, hoping the words would come together to mean something in a way I hadn't appreciated.

It was a strategy I learned from Paul, an avid crossword player who often tore one out of the newspaper and kept it in his shirt pocket to be completed by the end of the day—in ink.

"Start with the big words you know and fill them in," he told me when I tried to do one on my own. "The rest will be obvious once you get far enough along." It didn't work for me.

The night before, when we had set the alarm, I groaned in anticipation of the day. Paul was an "early to bed and early to rise" kind of person while I was a "sleep whenever and get up when you have to" girl, but the next day I would need to be up at six, preparing to travel to Philadelphia for a student's dissertation defense. When I dragged myself from bed and went to the kitchen, Paul was on the sofa with sections of the newspaper spread around him. He looked worse than I felt.

"Gosh, you look really beat," I said, pausing with the coffee pot in one hand and my empty cup in the other. "Are you okay?" His eyes were bloodshot, and his face sagged with fatigue. He held out his cup and I went over to fill it.

"I've been up since two," he said.

He was a notorious insomniac, even with plenty of sleep-promoting medication and especially when he had a lot going on at work. The night before as we ate dinner, he talked at length about not being able to "keep up" with younger associates who came into the firm equipped with both legal knowledge and technology skills.

"Just like Casey at bat, I'm striking out," he had said, and then quoted the entire "Mighty Casey Has Struck Out" poem.

Worries about his job were something we discussed frequently, and, as usual, I encouraged him to think about finding something less demanding or retiring altogether. As usual, he deflected my suggestions. He had to keep his job, he thought, to cover health care benefits and the cost of our children's on-going needs. It was hard to believe he was seriously concerned though, when he could cite a childhood poem from memory, smiling when finished.

After refilling his coffee cup that next morning, I listened to the familiar anxiety in his voice as he described the depositions awaiting him.

"Paul, why worry so much? You know you'll do fine—you always do."

Did he even hear me? He snapped the newspaper together and stood up, moving toward the kitchen from the family room and walking right into the lightweight love seat angled next to the sofa. He knocked it over but didn't pause to pick it up.

"Paul—what's going on?"

There had been an edge to my voice almost like the one I used to command attention from the children or Lacey. It was the same tone I used years ago when Paul smashed out the rear window of our hatchback while trying to slam it shut on a stroller—and then drove away, leaving the parking lot littered with glittering glass fragments. I used it a few years after that when he fell on a glass coffee table and shattered it, and again when he walked by an end table in the family room and somehow knocked it over and broke one of the pair of pottery lamps I had been proud to buy on sale. In fact, just a month earlier, he had slipped while taking a shower in a hotel bathroom and hit his head, hard, on a massive granite countertop. Then, I had been horrified by the fall's impact, confused about how it had happened and scared it would have fatal consequences.

In the same way he had responded to those other accidents, Paul looked at me blankly, as if he had no idea what I was talking about or why I was upset. He pointed at his open briefcase, which was stuffed with legal files.

"Cheryl, this is a big day. All my subpoenas could be ignored."

"But you just knocked over the love seat."

He glanced over his shoulder and shrugged.

"What's going on?" I pressed, trying to figure out why he still hadn't picked the loveseat up. "Are you feeling okay?"

"I'm just getting my hearing aid."

I righted the sofa and cradled my coffee cup in my hand, studying him. "I'm worried about you."

"I'll be fine," he said, as if I had convinced him. Still a bit unsettled, I headed to the bedroom to get ready for my day and hoped that, as usual, Paul's worries would turn out to be unfounded.

As I was getting into the shower, there was a sound in the distance like one that heralded a sudden thunderstorm. I hesitated, waiting to hear more or see a flash of lightening, but there was only silence. Pulling on my robe, I went back to the family room and looked around. Most likely, Paul was in the basement, ironing a shirt, but he may have gone upstairs to find the suit he would wear to court that day.

"Paul?" I took a few more steps toward the kitchen. "Paul!"

The door between the family room and the basement of our old house was quirky; the size of a regular door but split in half lengthwise so that the panels could swing open and shut separately, saloon-style. Through a sliver of space between them, I could see that the stair light was on.

When I pushed the doors open, Lacey was there, quivering on the top step. She scurried by me, and I went down.

Paul was sprawled on the bottom landing. His arms and legs were flopped out like those of a young boy floating down a country stream on a hot summer afternoon, and his face was serene.

He's dead, I said to myself, but that couldn't be true. It had only been minutes since our conversation upstairs, but when I tried to rouse him, he didn't respond. That's when I called 911, dropped into prayer position, and, taking a deep breath in, sealed my lips over his.

———

"Ladies, Cardiopulmonary Resuscitation may be the most important skill of your nursing career," my freshman instructor had said. I could almost see how I had looked then, kneeling over Resusci-Annie, the rite-of-passage mannequin every health care professional practiced on. Each new job I would take after graduation required CPR competence, defined by the ability to keep Annie's "heart" pumping and her "lungs" breathing. My friends and I had rolled our eyes at each other when the teacher's back was turned, probably a combination of nervous anticipation over really having to revive someone and the ridiculousness of the hard plastic doll with no human features.

Despite working for years as a nurse, my instructor was wrong. I never had to do CPR on a patient, even though I participated in plenty of codes where we worked in other ways to bring a patient back to life. There was a chance to practice my skills when a man who collapsed leaving church one Sunday led me to crouch on the hard pavement in my heels, stockings, and dress and do chest compressions while a physician who was also leaving the service came forward and did mouth-to-mouth breathing. After a few rounds, we were successful.

That was not happening with Paul.

The 911 operator kept up a steady dialogue as I continued CPR and prayed for the ambulance to come quickly. Just when the few minutes that had passed since I discovered my husband lifeless on the basement floor began to feel like hours of desperate effort, the distant yowl of a siren grew louder and louder until the air vibrated. Heavy footsteps pounded overhead, and my heroes, three emergency squad personnel, rushed down the steps.

"They're here," I told the operator. "Thank you so much."

I punched my cellphone off and stepped back as the crew took over, snapping open equipment bags and tearing apart packages of IV fluids and an airway. In another lifetime, I would have been part of their team.

"We have an unresponsive male," one of the medics said into his walkie-talkie, continuing to hand over supplies with his other. "Heart rhythm normal but no spontaneous respirations."

Within seconds, they had Paul hooked up to a heart monitor and were squeezing an Ambu breathing bag to deliver oxygen. By then, I had called Joe, our youngest son, who lived a short distance away. He must have driven over the speed limit because he arrived as the paramedics jostled a stretcher with his grey-faced comatose father strapped to it up the basement steps and toward the ambulance.

"Joe, I think Dad is dead," I said.

His face, already pale and stretched tight with stress, grew whiter, and his hands clenched into fists. We jumped into his car and followed the ambulance to the hospital ER, taking the same route I drove every morning to work.

In less than an hour, the ER team had started a ventilator, IV, and catheter, wheeling Paul in and out of his cubicle for X-rays and scans of the inside of his brain. Joe and I huddled together in the family waiting room, waiting for news.

"Cheryl?"

The hospital chaplain came in after seeing my last name on the patient board by the nurses' station. He was a kind man who had no words to comfort us, but I appreciated his willingness to try—the first of many of my coworkers to show up and offer sympathy.

After receiving all the test results, a neurology resident came to us, his eyes sorrowful. Introducing himself, he held out a piece of paper with a black and white image of a brain on it. Even untrained someone would be able to see that there much more black than white.

"Your husband had a massive cerebral hemorrhage," he said, looking from Joe to me and then back again. "We can do surgery, but he's still bleeding, and chances are, he'll never be the same. He'd need to be in a nursing home with a ventilator."

Paul and I had discussed death and dying a lot—maybe even more than most couples who have been married a long time. We debated it in the context of faith (me) and fear (him). In the last year, it had been an even more frequent topic, perhaps because of the research I was involved in or because three people we cared about deeply had passed away.

"That's weird. Dad and I talked about this not too long ago," Joe said. "But then it was a big joke." His face still had the stricken expression of a severe trauma survivor.

"What's the likelihood he could recover?" I asked the resident. "He wouldn't want to live if it meant being a vegetable." I nodded toward the room where Paul was secured to a bed with machines and monitors in a half-circle around him.

Medicine is all about likelihoods. Will a new medication with side effects help a patient more than the marginally effective old one? If risky abdominal surgery is performed and several tumors removed, what are the chances the cancer will go away for good? What are the odds of an extremely premature infant surviving intact with vigorous medical treatment? It's the most maddening questions we try to answer with numbers because there are no clear ethical choices.

The resident's lips pressed into a line. "I'd say none, really."

Joe's brown eyes, so like my own, shut for a moment. They were wet with unshed tears, and although he was twenty-three and a father himself, I longed to hug him hard and reassure him that everything was going to be okay. Maybe it would be more for my comfort than his, but as I started to reach out, the resident spoke again.

"We'll send him up to NICU so everyone can say good-bye."

I was familiar with the Neurologic Intensive Care Unit. Paul's father, Joe Senior, had died in the room right next to the one they admitted Paul to, which provided an eerie foretaste of what was to come.

People were kind. The warden at the county prison who was a friend of Paul's allowed Ellen, who was incarcerated at the time, to come to the hospital, shackled and wearing a beige jumpsuit. She was escorted by two guards, a protocol reserved for the only the worst of personal crises.

My family had arrived in short order, along with Paul's mother and brother. Others trickled in, including my brother, who left directly from work in Baltimore to drive to the medical center. The NICU space was so small each new arrival caused a pulse of shock to ping from person to person like some kind of emotional radar.

The physicians and nurses were supportive, too. This was a drill they knew well, and I was an employee at their institution, making me one of their own. They checked in on us frequently, and nodded understanding when I told them we were ready. One of the physicians even came in and sat next to me on the bed.

"You're making the right decision," he said. "There were some disturbing things on his scans."

At the time, I assumed those "disturbing things" were the flood of blood that obliterated my husband's brain, but later, when I got his medical records, I learned there was a huge mass on Paul's left kidney. "Needs immediate attention and referral to nephrology," the doctor wrote.

Once the decision had been made to stop the machines, I insisted that Paul be given a final injection of morphine, even though the physician told me it wouldn't really have an effect.

"I don't care. It will make me feel better," I said, not explaining my worries about Paul's low threshold for pain. Even though he was unresponsive, he might be in agony due to the pressure of swollen brain tissue pushing against the thick bone of his skull—how would I know?

In another scenario, I might have told the doctor about the

time when I administered what ended up being a final dose of morphine to a beloved patient. Maybe I would have asked him how he knew there really was no impact to the bolus of morphine since patients usually die afterwards. Instead, I moved to the head of the bed and watched as the nurse administered the medicine through the IV line. Then she silently and reverently disconnected the ventilator and removed the heart monitor leads.

After she finished, I climbed into the bed and wedged myself next to Paul.

"You know I love you, and I'm going to miss you so much," I whispered.

I kept repeating the words, even though it was a lie. I wasn't going to miss him because I fully expected to go home and find him there, stretched out on the leather sofa we bought because it reminded him of his childhood baseball glove. I would flop down next to him, and we would talk about the events of our day as if nothing had ever happened.

2. hershey, pa
2009-2010

There are signs at either end of town that claim Hershey, PA, is "The Sweetest Place on Earth." For me, it became the saddest place after Paul died because there were reminders him everywhere. Just down the street was the grocery store where he bought ribs to cook on the barbecue, and within walking distance was the library where he spent hours browsing through magazines and regularly got his card revoked for unpaid fines. When I took the Chocolate Avenue route home from work, I passed by our favorite restaurant and saw the pool where we swam laps outside in the summer.

Tourists describe our little town as "charming," and locals who love it refer to "the chocolate bubble" that keeps us encapsulated from the world, but within its boundaries there are few secrets. When my daughter developed an eating disorder that would lead to years of struggle, the news spread quickly. Other mothers at her school began to treat me like a pariah, as if fearful their children would "catch" whatever she had. Whenever I went to the pharmacy or the gym, I would try to avoid the curious looks that were often followed by questions about her from people who had never said a word to me before.

Within hours of Paul arriving by ambulance at the medical center complex that was also my employer, my coworkers showed up at the NICU, alerted by the social network that was faster than any email. It was kind but awkward; I will never forget the sight of the damp spots of my tears on the crisp blue of my boss's shirt and the gentleness of my colleagues as they asked how they could be of help. Food showed up at my house daily, and for weeks after his death and when I arrived on campus, it felt like everyone was giving me looks of pity. When someone sent me a copy of his obituary in an unmarked manila envelope through interoffice mail, it was the only time I broke down, partly out of grief and partly from confusion.

Of course, I/we could have moved away any number of times and avoided the spotlight of unwanted fame on our family, but we never quite had the energy to do it. In the year after Paul died, I vowed to sell the house where we spent over a decade and relocate to a place where no one knew me as the "Mother of Ellen" or "Wife of the attorney who fell down the steps and died."

His death prompted me to lead my off-work hours hidden away in my own little niche—even if it was an unhappy place. I found that I could navigate familiar and predictable micro distances: half a mile to the gas station, one mile to work or a movie and about the same for a good-enough restaurant, knowing that I could then retreat to my bedroom. Before long, more of my time was spent inside my house than beyond it.

"You're secluding yourself," Joe said at one point in the early months after his dad died.

In a haze of medication-induced sedation, I wanted to mumble, "Why yes, I am, thank you very much," but didn't. Worrying him was the last thing I needed to add to both of our lists of troubles; instead I roused from my bed, went back to work, and pretended everything was okay for a few days. "Okay" until early evening, when I could grab my white dog, Lacey, and barricade myself for the next twelve hours, sailing through night dreams in a mist of drugs and memories that would get me through to the magical one-year mark.

I believed in the "one year milestone" because early in my career, I had been assigned to teach "Death & Dying," a course that got passed around our faculty like a hot potato. No one wanted to teach it, but those of us who were young and/or on tenure track had no choice.

"It's a killer. No pun intended," one of the senior professors told me. My first time through the class, I understood what she meant.

It was a rare elective for upperclassmen scheduled on Thursdays from 5-8 p.m., a time, I later learned, when many students believed the weekend should begin. While my 100+ coeds sat in old-fashioned fold down seats with wooden tablet style desktops fastened to the right side, their classmates were drifting down to the bars that lined College Avenue or heading home for a three day break.

After the first time through the course there was a rhythm to teaching it that felt natural. I remember responding to questions about how people deal with grief with the same wisdom: "It takes time. Sometimes, after an especially serious loss, it might be twelve months or more before a person recovers, but there's generally a slow progression forward that builds momentum."

There was always a cynic in the crowd, ready to counter any claim or opinion.

"How do you know that? Does somebody actually sit down and measure out the time it takes to get over losing someone or something you love?"

Usually, the students who asked questions like that sat close to the front, far from the sleepers and socializers along the back wall. I appreciated challengers because they made class interesting, and, I like to think, brought out my best teaching efforts.

"What do you all say? Some of you have experienced death or a significant loss. How did you grieve?" I would cast a sweeping gaze from one side of the drab classroom to the other, my eyebrows raised.

The question about grieving was always a lightning bolt, inspiring students who hadn't made eye contact with me all semester to speak up. In front of their peers, most of whom were strangers, juniors and seniors would share deeply personal stories.

"I had cancer as a child, but recovered after everyone thought I would die," one young woman said, showing a scar where her port for chemotherapy used to be. "Now it seems like it was all a bad dream."

"My friends and I were in a canoe accident, and I nearly drowned. It was one of those near-death experiences," another student shared, pausing as the room went quiet. "I can still relive every one of those last seconds."

"I had an abortion. I didn't think of it as my child dying at the time, but now I do," said a girl near the front without flinching. "I think of it every day."

There were losses of an unimaginable magnitude: family and friends killed by car accidents and drug overdoses. There were suicides, homicides, and the inevitable deaths of a beloved grandparent. I learned to bring a box of tissues to the grief class so I would have something concrete to offer those who wept.

After I left that university, I collaborated with a research team on a study of end-of-life decision-making. Again, I found myself listening to many stories about past or pending deaths. I took comfort in what I thought I knew: death was a finite event, a moment in time marked by a certificate and filed away, or a date engraved on a headstone.

Teaching and research weren't the only things that influenced my beliefs about grief. My family hadn't suffered many immediate or unexpected losses by the time I graduated from nursing school, but then, in my early twenties, as a nurse I cared for Mike, a young man injured in a serious motorcycle accident. He was about the same age as my younger brother.

Mike was admitted to the ICU from the ER, attached to tubes and machines that kept air going in and out of his lungs and fluid circulating in his veins. I worked a double shift, which felt like being part of a military maneuver, to preserve Mike's life: the doctors would bark out orders and I would run to fulfill them. I stayed at the bedside for most of the time Mike was in the ICU, spoke to his parents and siblings, and listened when his pastor said a prayer over his unconscious soul.

That afternoon, when I returned to work, Mike's bed was empty and clean sheets were tucked into the mattress.

"Miss Miller, why are you crying?" the head nurse asked, when she saw me wipe away tears after being told that Mike died not long after I left that morning.

"He was just a teenager....and we tried so hard," I said.

"Your job is done," she said.

"Should I go to his funeral? I really got to know his family."

"Let them grieve and move on. In a year, they'll be fine," she said.

That's what I continued to believe when I sat by the bedside or visited dying patients as part of my clinical work in the years before I went on to teaching. Once death occurred, I thought, there was little more for me to do. Just as I would go on to tell my university students, I told newly bereaved family and friends that things would generally straighten themselves out and people would "move on."

Then my husband died, and things got worse instead of better. His health was good, but somehow, he fell and hit his head so hard blood flooded his brain like a tsunami. A month passed and then six. At nine months, I felt worse than I had in the week after his death. What was wrong?

As the one-year anniversary approached, I was still waiting for the heavy cloud that had settled over my life to clear. I was tired of being "Grieving Cheryl," a woman who seemed to attract bigger crises as each month passed. Standing in front of a hundred-plus students all those years ago, there was no reason to believe my husband would die at the age of 56 and I would discover what grief was really about. He rarely missed a day of work, always came home at the same time, and met the demands of parenting and husbanding with fairly good grace. Most days, he probably enjoyed his job more than I did mine, despite its drawbacks. He was predictable and comfortable, making it easy to imagine spending our last years together in a nursing home close enough for children and grandchildren to visit.

In the wake of his dying, the life he and I created unraveled before me as if it never existed. My oldest son, who was in the military, was yanked out of Afghanistan by the Red Cross to attend the funeral, without his pregnant wife's consent or my suggestion, which is apparently military protocol. He arrived too late for the service and his wife was furious.

Her first words to me when she walked in my kitchen after flying across the country to meet up with her husband were, "I hope you're satisfied. Now he can't come home when the baby is born."

My good old girl, Texan sister-in-law was nearby and swooped in to comfort me when I fled from the room.

"That girl needs to learn when to hold her words," she said, but I knew there would be more bitterness and many accusations in the months to follow—I just couldn't have imagined how intense they would be.

My daughter, who was permitted to come to the memorial service in a regular dress, was swept back to prison as soon as it ended and had to grieve alone. A week later, I was in court for her sentencing. The judge, whom I knew from previous hearings, was a grandfatherly man with a surprisingly kind smile.

"I knew your dad, and I believe you can do better than you have so far. I'm sending you for rehabilitation," he said. Unable to thank him personally, I asked her attorney to convey my gratitude to the judge and share my belief that this time, my daughter had real motivation to change her life.

She completed the drug treatment program and then went to a halfway house where she got caught shooting heroin. That led her back to jail and then to a work release program she eloped from.

For weeks, I had no idea where in the country she was and undertook a massive Internet campaign to try and locate her. My notoriety from my first book, which described the experiences of mothers of troubled teens, generated a plethora of emails, some consoling and some bizarre. For a brief time, I thought my daughter might be in Alabama with a woman who knew her from rehab.

As the days went on with no idea of her real location, I was on the verge of a total breakdown.

"Let's go put up fliers in Philadelphia," my much younger sister, Beth, suggested. "You said she might be there."

It felt hopeful, so I agreed, and we drove to South Philadelphia and posted fliers with her picture on every street corner. We trolled the neighborhoods of the Italian district and interviewed any bartender or street person who would talk to us.

"She has friends in the area," I said, over and over.

In a sequence of events that felt as unreal as Paul's death, my daughter finally contacted me at work to say she was "staying" with a man who lived in a bad neighborhood in Harrisburg. My coworker and friend was able to trace the call, enabling me to notify the police and go to her rescue. It turned out that she had been kidnapped and was being held against her will—had I not thought to call the authorities, I might have been grabbed, too.

"Tell your daughter to stay out of this neighborhood," one of the officers who met me at the place where she was held said, eyeing my dress and high heels. If only parenting was that simple.

She returned to jail—not the kind depicted in *Orange is the New Black,* but a county jail, where security was tight. Each time I went to see her, the female guard seemed to frisk me a bit more thoroughly than necessary, and then grunt her dismissal. I would sit in the waiting room with other visitors until we were admitted to another room, three at a time. We would sit on one side of a bulletproof plastic window and our loved ones on the other. Most of the time she cried and there was no way to even hold and hug her.

My youngest son, his wife, and their daughter, moved in with me shortly after Paul died. It was a show of support but went badly from the beginning. None of us were doing well. My coping strategy was to hide out in my bedroom, where I had moved a TV and computer, and curl up with Lacey. My son and his wife went to work, invited friends over, and took care of their daughter on the other side of my bedroom door. Eventually, they began looking for a place of their own and moved out, with my blessing. It was then that I realized how big and empty the house truly was.

Those weren't my only problems. Immediately after Paul's death, something triggered the IRS, leading to hours on the phone with sympathetic spokespeople who nonetheless made it clear my wages could be garnished to pay taxes I didn't know were due—that had been Paul's job. Every day when the mailman delivered thick official envelopes with long forms that requested more information, I berated myself for being so uninvolved during the years of our marriage.

One time, I found myself sobbing to a person on the IRS hotline. "I don't know anything about unpaid taxes. My husband just died..." I had to hold the phone away from my ear and take a second to stifle my tears.

"Oh, you poor thing," the man on the other end said. "I'm a widower myself. I know how you feel. It's terrible."

Forgive me for plunging through so many "and thens," but one of the first things I learned about grief was that there's no nice way to tell the story, even though you are compelled to repeat it again and again to anyone who is willing to listen. That first post-death year felt like an action movie full of explosions and violence that resulted in jolt after jolt of unbelievable hurt—and I couldn't stop rehashing the details, as if that would make them fit into what I told students was "a cogent narrative."

"It helps to listen," I had said in one of the Death & Dying classes, focusing on the earnest faces in the first row who wrote down just about every word I said. "A person who is grieving needs to make sense of what has happened and create a cogent narrative about it." When I became a widow, I discovered that the presence of empathetic listeners only made me cry harder.

There were ironies and kindnesses alongside the pain. As a serial Weight Watcher since the birth of my youngest child, I had never quite reached my goal of losing those final ten or fifteen pounds. After Paul died, thirty pounds fell from my frame in nearly as many days, turning me skeletal and sapping my already depleted will to live. Family and friends commented on my "diet" and seemed not to believe my insistence that the weight loss, for a change, was not intentional.

"You're coming to the beach house with us," my coworker Jeanne said one afternoon at work. Along with Deb and Linda, two other colleagues, we drove south for a three-day vacation. In an attempt to motivate me, they seemed to eat hourly.

"Let's get milkshakes," one of them would say, pointing at a fast-food store.

"This place has great seafood," was the excuse to have dinner at a local restaurant.

"Chinese!" prompted a takeout lunch.

"Deb is making breakfast," Jeanne said in a low voice on our last day there. "Eat so you don't hurt her feelings."

Their efforts were so transparently tender that I did my best, but a week later, I was back to choking down Power Bars in the solitude of my bedroom, allowing Lacey to lick the sticky residue off my fingers.

I took another trip not long after Paul died, flying to Florida to see my best friend, Susan, whom I met during my Resusci-Annie days. In the airport, she walked past me, and when I called out, she looked bewildered.

"Cheryl, how much weight have you lost?" she asked after hugging me as if I was a piece of fragile bone china.

She, too, tried to entice me into eating, and I agreed to try, but the good intentions faded away when I returned home. To the house where Paul wasn't. To a daughter in prison and two sons who were struggling in different but significant ways. To a job that seemed pointless. To continue my new life as a widow.

Widow. Each time I said the word, it felt like I was talking about someone else.

———

All I wanted was a few months of peace—not even good things, just no more bad ones.

"Don't think about being happy," Paul had told me shortly after we met. "That's my philosophy. I just want the absence of grief. You know, to be not unhappy."

In the months after he died, I was worse than "not unhappy," trapped in an alien life without a husband whose love I never doubted, forcing myself to show up at a job I used to be good at, and in the midst of a disastrous failed book deal that my agent might never forgive. Then there was my first post-Paul romance, a spectacular fail...

During a phone call check-in from Beth, I detailed all those problems, and then tried to put in words exactly how I felt. I didn't need to—she and I had the kind of innate understanding of each other only sisters possess.

"I've tried everything—therapy, books, booze, romance, travel.... Paul's been dead almost a year now, and it feels like things are worse instead of better, and still going downhill."

In the silence, I could feel her processing my rant. "That sucks. But I did warn you about getting caught up in a big love affair so soon. Don't you remember that talk we had on New Year's? I told you he was the first man you had been with since Paul and that you needed to be careful. I said the same to him."

"I remember you crying and begging him not to hurt me." That image made me wince because she wasn't the only one who had cautioned me against getting seriously involved with a man who had a reputation for breaking hearts.

"Hmm." Although we're seventeen years apart, we make the same sounds when thinking out loud. "Well, what about a clairvoyant?"

"You must be kidding. Maybe you don't have a problem with woo-woo, but I do. I would never go to a clairvoyant."

"It's not 'woo-woo'—there are things that can't be explained in this world, Cheryl. Anyway, the woman I know is a Christian. She prays before she does a reading," Beth said, as if adding in religion made a clairvoyant more credible.

I shook my head even though she couldn't see it. As a scientist, I believed everything was explainable. Even when your hypothesis failed, it still proved something—you were wrong, and you kept trying until you got data-driven correct answers.

Beth, a musician, easily accepted the intangible. Almost nothing seemed too bizarre to her: making body casts of pregnant women, accepting the label of "witch" from one of her neighbors, and using Ouija boards, tarot cards, and runes to discern direction. Although I've never seen a crystal ball in her house, I wouldn't rule out there being one.

We overlapped in the area of spirituality, though. Despite our age difference, we had been brought up in the same religious environment, which required church attendance, baptism, and confirmation. Not surprisingly, we expressed our faiths differently—she was a tree-hugger, I was a church-goer—but we still believed in most of the doctrine we learned from the Lutheran church.

Not long after sharing my sorrows with Beth, I remembered Amtrak and the ease of travel it offered. I had my own rewards card and knew the timetable to and from New York City by heart, traveling by train frequently for work or a weekend away. As the one-year anniversary of Paul's death loomed closer, I decided to make an adult attempt to run away from home. It would be a long trip, and maybe, if some other town or city looked better to me than enchanted Hershey, Pennsylvania, I wouldn't come back.

harrisburg, pa
the daily pennsylvanian
june 2010

Balancing what must have been about fifty pounds of luggage, I inched down the pockmarked steel steps that led from the station to the train platform. It was like trying to walk on the steepest part of a roller coaster track with people close in front of you and behind; one wrong move and there would be a disaster.

"You'd think all the fancy senators who come back and forth every day would pony up some money for renovations," a fellow traveler observed once. "But this deathtrap hasn't changed in ages."

That comment was made long before I felt vulnerable about my ability to navigate life, much less a triple flight of stairs. I ended up grabbing onto the rail, and then, when everyone else had passed, edged forward as if playing the children's game of "baby steps." When I reached the bottom, my stomach clenched so tight I felt lightheaded.

Don't go, an inner voice whispered. *Something terrible will happen while you're away.*

I took a deep breath and held it for a few seconds. I had given birth three times, completed triathlons, and earned tenure. I could do this.

The cautionary voice was insistent. *What if something happens to you? No one will know if you get hurt or attacked or lost. There's no Paul to check in with now, you know.*

In front of me, a herd of people shifted back and forth, angling for the best position to board the train when it arrived. The packet of tickets in my hand was stamped "Nonrefundable," but for a moment, I stuffed it in my pocket and edged away from the treacherous steps.

Then I heard it.

The platform trembled as the engine charged into the station, airbrakes shrieking. The train struggled to a stop and the doors hissed open. Passengers surged out, pushing through the wall of new travelers and charging up the steps.

"Let 'em out folks, let 'em out. Coming through," the conductor shouted, wading into the crowd's midst. Only his hand could be seen, bobbing like a life buoy above a sea of people.

Behind him, an elderly lady with a walker appeared, slowly easing across the gap between the train and the platform, her head bent. She paused after making the transition, looking up to smile at the people around her as if assuring us she was okay.

"Nana!"

The shrill voice of a child called from the top of the steps I had just descended where friends and family waited for passengers. The old woman came to a complete stop, squinted in the direction of the exit, and took one hand off her walker to wave.

"I'm coming, Mary," she said, and then turned her attention back to the task at hand: navigating the platform.

Once she was a few steps beyond the train doors, the boarding passengers swirled around her in a rush to push inside. How would she ever make it up those steps? Was someone planning to carry her?

"I need the elevator," she told the conductor. "And some nice young man dressed just like you has my suitcase."

"Yes ma'am. He's meeting us there." The conductor held up a walkie-talkie. "Right around that corner."

He pointed in the direction of a sign labeled "Elevator." After hundreds of trips on this train, I never knew there was an alternative to the steps.

As the conductor hovered at her side and "Nana" made her way forward, my heart began to feel like a fist punching the inside of my chest. I wanted a kindly conductor to guide me to the right place and make sure my luggage arrived safely and there was a happy child to greet me at the end of my trip.

The voice inside my head was impatient. *That's right. You're a little old to be running away from home. Maybe that worked when you were twenty, but not now. You need to hop on that elevator and get back to Hershey, where you're safe, just like Nana.*

I looked up at The Daily Pennsylvanian, a train that travels one of the busiest and oldest routes in the country, making the trip from Pittsburgh to New York City on a route that a sister train, The Keystoner, shared at other times of the day and for shorter distances. I had ridden both trains eastward so often my frequent traveler card contributed thousands of points toward past fares.

"YougointoPittsburgh?" The conductor drawled from behind me. The platform was empty but for me, and his "Nana" persona was gone—I was holding up his train, and he wasn't happy about it.

I thought about saying "No," and doing exactly what the inner voice had suggested: flee back to Hershey, where my bedroom retreat waited along with a little white dog who was always thrilled to see me. There I could hide out indefinitely, waiting for my journey through grief to be complete.

Then a side of me that had gotten me through competitions in school and life spoke. "Absolutely not." This trip would prove that I could be strong again. I would stop hiding out in a comfortable small world of my own making and my mourning would end. I would become, finally, a brand-new version of myself: "Coping Cheryl."

"So, Paul is your anchor. He can stop you from drifting into dangerous territory, but he can also weigh you down," my therapist had suggested one time when our marriage was in serious trouble, and I sought her counsel.

"You're right," I said. "But I usually think about the weighing me down part."

Standing on the Harrisburg platform just like the deer I sometimes caught in my headlights while driving on the back roads of Hershey, her comment echoed across the years. For the duration of my marriage, it had been easy to travel around the world for work, attending conferences, meetings, and workshops in new, faraway places knowing Paul was at home, waiting for my return.

Now, there would be no one to text when I reached my destination safely. No one to chat with during lunch or recap the day with as I made my way across the country. If a random murderer or rapist grabbed me or I fell onto the tracks and ended up comatose in a distant hospital, my best hope of anyone finding out about it was a smart detective.

The conductor bellowed, "Pitts-burgh, all aboard for Pittsburgh," a signal to me and a couple to my right who had just scurried down the stairs and were kissing good-bye.

I took another deep breath just like I did when trying to swim the length of a pool underwater, shifted my purse, backpack, and carry-on into position, and moved forward. Maneuvering around the conductor and through the train's door, I didn't look back as yet another part of my life fell away.

———

Being the last person to board the train meant there were no empty double seats. As the car began to nudge forward, I realized the nearest available spot was the one right next to me, in the first row.

"Anyone sitting here?" I asked the man in the seat next to the window, who was staring at me with a faintly creased forehead.

"Nope. Help yourself," he said.

I plopped down, still holding my backpack and suitcase, trying not to inhale. We were only a few feet from the two bathrooms right inside the entrance, one handicapped and one regular. Both had metal doors that I knew would make a loud noise each time they were rolled opened or shut, and if they weren't latched properly, they would slide-slam continuously, offering all its sights and smells.

Great. Not only will you be listening to those doors and smelling pink industrial soap for the next six hours, you're also stuck next to a man who looks very strange, in a seat without a dropdown tray to put your stuff on. The inner voice again.

It was the man part of that equation that alarmed me most. My initial glance in his direction registered something that was not quite right. My seatmate was about my age, and, with a slight squint, he could be an older Richard Gere in a very muscular body, but he had no device to listen to, no laptop to peck on, and no book or other reading material. There was no briefcase or newspaper tucked on the floor next to him, no jacket draped across his lap, and no used ticket stub peeking out of the pocket of his polo shirt. He was sitting as if frozen, so still I shifted away in my seat for fear I would accidentally touch him.

The conductor who had urged me to board was coming down the aisle, so I pulled my tickets back out. Although I had sorted through them the night before, I couldn't locate the right page for my Harrisburg to Pittsburgh leg of the journey. Had it somehow fallen out? What if I had lost it?

Are you surprised, Cheryl? Anything that can go wrong for you, will. If you've learned anything this last year, that's it, my inner cynic commented.

"Can I help you?" The conductor held out his hand, and after flipping through the booklet, whipped a hole punch off his belt, clicked one of the pages, tore off half of another, and returned it to me.

My seatmate looked over. "That looks like a hefty trip. Special occasion?"

"Just a trip, no real purpose," I said.

The conductor, who seemed to hesitate as if wondering the same thing, slammed the handicapped bathroom door shut and ambled away. My seatmate studied me for a second.

"Where to?"

"Across the country and back."

"Really? Just because you can? Are you writing a book?"

That made me raise my eyebrows and look sideways at him. "I guess anything can be a book. How about you? What do you do?"

"I'm a consultant to the military."

He looked away as if interested in the sights beyond his window, but there was nothing casual about his demeanor. In fact, I got the sense that he had his ears trained on the chatter of conversation taking place behind us.

"I am from Pakistan. Do you know it?" The voice, heavily accented, belonged to a middle-aged man in a turban and robe seated directly behind me. I had noticed him when I sat down, already in the midst of an animated dialogue with his seatmate, a nondescript man who might have been in his forties.

Before the fellow could reply to the question, the Pakistani continued. "It's a county with many problems. I come from a village, very small village in the mountains. Do you know what it is like to live in a small place? Wait, before you answer, let me tell you my experiences."

Without pause, he continued to speak, posing questions but then launching into another monologue before his seatmate could answer them.

"What kind of consultant?" I turned back to my seatmate.

His head seemed to be tipped slightly toward the speaker behind us. "Weapons, things like that. But tell me, why are you going cross-country now? By the way, I'm Lee."

"I'm Cheryl. I take the train a lot and just wanted to go on a trip." I shrugged, and then realized I was still holding my tickets. I tucked them in my purse, pulled out my cellphone, and checked for messages or email. My inbox still held the last text I had sent Paul, "Can you bring the blanket in from the trunk of your car when you get home?" If I had known it would be my last message to him, I would have added, "I love you," but that was something we had stopped saying to each other only a few years into the marriage.

Still, I had whispered it in his ear right before the NICU doctor disconnected the ventilator that was the only thing keeping him alive, believing he might somehow hear or sense my feelings even when I saw no sign this was the case. From the seconds after I found him until he was officially pronounced, Paul had not responded in any way to the world around him.

Every night in my bedroom when I lit candles in his memory, I tried to convince myself that I still loved him, but the truth was that I was angry. My husband had not been the reliable worker and steady father I thought he was. He had not put me and our family at the top of his priority list as I had, and on the train, for the first time, that realization sank in. I was not like the gently grieving widows I had met time and again in my nursing career—I was bitter and furious.

"My late husband, John, named for the apostle, was a saint himself," I remembered one of my long ago patients telling me. Her name was Virginia and she lived in rural Pennsylvania, recently discharged from the hospital for treatment of her chronic heart problems; I was there to admit her to our home health agency. She lived alone in a trailer at the end of a long dirt lane and was widowed for nearly a year, but John's presence was everywhere: smiling pictures of him were propped on table tops and his collection of baseball hats still hung on one wall. The pickup truck in the backyard was his, and the ancient dog, Rufus, who could barely wobble over to sniff at my legs while I sat filling out paperwork, was "John's dog."

Like so many other older women I would meet, for the rest of my time with Virginia, she would always talk about John in a favorable way. The trials and troubles that came into their lives (like bankruptcy and the stepdaughter he refused to speak to) were forgotten, and he became the doer of good deeds and creator of positive emotions, more flawless and revered in death than any person could have been in life. After lifetimes with men who were sometimes difficult, many of the elderly widows I came to care for had a partial amnesia, remembering more good than bad.

I couldn't talk about Paul that way. His secret life, which had emerged in the week after he died, left me feeling both betrayed and vengeful—not the emotions a recently bereaved spouse is supposed to feel. When people said, "Your husband was such a nice person," or "Your husband was a special man," it was all I could do to masquerade my real feelings, give a wan smile, and say, "Thank you." In some ways, it was a rerun of the situation our whole family faced when my daughter struggled through years of disordered eating and addictions: no one printed it in the local newspaper, but somehow, the details of her hospitalizations and incarcerations seemed to be such public knowledge that total strangers didn't hesitate to approach me and ask disturbingly personal questions.

Perhaps that is why I felt such "grief shame"; I wasn't honoring my husband in the way it seemed a surviving spouse was supposed to, even if s/he didn't feel that way. How many times had I heard patients or my own friends and family caution against "speaking ill of the dead"?

I was in many ways an expert on death and dying, yet I was failing at widowhood. I couldn't accept the advice I gave others and "take care of myself" with good nutrition and exercise because my appetite and motivation had evaporated. I couldn't plan for the future, because what had happened in the past shattered the framework of who Paul and I had been for the last twenty-eight years. I couldn't gather happy memories to console me, because the betrayal that simmered underneath them changed everything they represented.

The only thing I could do was stay put until I decided to take the train trip. Professionals encourage those in the midst of grief to make no major changes for the first year after the death of a loved one, but that's not why I continued to live in our Hershey house and work in the same place. I simply didn't have the ability to search out somewhere new, find a home there, pack up all my belongings, and then move. Nor did I have the stamina to search for a new job that wasn't in the medical center where my husband had died and the note on his chart referred to me as "one of our own professors."

Inertia was an undercurrent during the year after Paul's death. He had been cremated as he wanted, but the urn with his ashes still sat in my bedroom. I hadn't even looked for the big headstone with both of our names on it that he had joked about, or located a double cemetery plot so we would, in his words, "be close forever." None of those things were that difficult, right? For me, they were as exhausting as running a marathon without any training.

lewistown
the daily pennsylvanian

By the time the train approached Lewistown, the little town where Paul and I had lived for five years, Lee had interrogated me thoroughly. He knew where I worked and what I liked about it, how many children I had and what they did, where I had gone to school, and more details about Paul than I would normally share with a stranger. Had anxiety led me to talk so freely with him, or was he just skilled at extracting information from strangers?

"I used to live there," I told him when the train halted to discharge and pick up passengers. "My kids would put pennies on the tracks and wait for the train to squash them flat. It was one of the exciting local things to do."

As I looked out the window at the shabby station and gently decaying town beyond it, the past was like a show on television that suddenly appeared. I could almost feel one of those pennies in my hand, a warm copper disc, and hear my children's excited shouts as they compared whose coin was the biggest.

We had been an unusual couple in Lewistown—the lawyer and his "working woman" wife—the first to invade "Pill Hill," a part of town where only physicians lived. Our house was a lovely ranch that we could barely afford, stretched out on top of a slope that would be matted with leaves we had to spend days raking at the end of fall. Not far from our front door was the bus stop, where our kids would meet with schoolmates from the neighborhood. A few blocks away, there was a small convenience store they could bike to and buy candy. It was idyllic in that "small town way" we would later see in Hershey, but it was also desperately poor. In reality, although the neighbors who commented about my career didn't realize it, most of the women in town worked, just not at Penn State University.

I was so novel that my older neighbor confessed to rising early so she could watch me each morning and observe what kind of clothing I wore to my job.

"Once those kids are on the bus, you really go flying off, don't you?" She shook her head. "Makes me tired to watch."

I didn't have time to be tired then. Our lives were on an upward trajectory, with Paul working at one of the town's few law firms and me driving 45 minutes to State College where I was a lowly instructor in the School of Nursing. The job was arduous, requiring me to be at clinical settings supervising students by 6:45 a.m. two mornings a week as well as lecturing and doing all the other things that went along with academic life. On top of that, I was finishing up my dissertation research so I could get my PhD and begin my "real career" on tenure track.

We were sure our (by then) three children would thrive in Lewistown, and they did. Since Paul's job was local, he was the one to pick them up from daycare and tote them to activities, which caused further comment from our neighbors. Surprisingly, for a man raised in a paternalistic military family with two brothers, he never complained about having to take on extra duties with the children.

"You should have seen the eyebrows go up when I got Ellen from ballet today," he told me one time. "I think I might be the first father ever allowed inside the dance studio."

I hadn't known when we moved there three years into our marriage that it would be the place where the first crisis in our relationship would occur, dividing our married life into "Before" and "After."

Of course, there had been plenty of times when I suspected something wasn't right with my husband's alcohol intake, but he was adept at convincing me I was wrong. Looking back, it seems stupidly naïve and gullible. One time, "Before" Lewistown, I had discovered an empty gin bottle under the front seat of his car when I drove it to Temple University in North Philly, where I was taking classes. I brought it into the house when I returned home and handed it to him.

"How did this get in your car?"

Paul didn't even blink, shrugging a dismissal. "Somebody broke into my car and put it there."

"The car was locked."

"You were in Philadelphia. Anything can happen there." He

had walked away then and I had let him.

There had always been six packs completely downed every Friday night and the fifth of Scotch that disappeared within two weeks of being purchased for "special occasions." He explained that the beer drinking was "just relaxing," and the Scotch bottle hadn't really been full when I first looked at it.

His excuses were always on the borderline of plausible, and had he been staying out late at bars, missing work because of a hangover, or crashing our cars, I might have pushed further, but none of those things happened. He looked perfectly normal and did all the things a responsible husband was supposed to do.

Then came the black-out that erased all doubts.

———

The children and I had come home from swimming on a Saturday afternoon and discovered him on the sofa, just about comatose. The harder I tried to rouse him, the more irritable he got. Still in a state of denial, I attributed his behavior to stress and fatigue, herding the kids off to the porch/playroom so they wouldn't ask questions.

Paul didn't come to bed that night and didn't rouse when Joe woke up crying with an earache. Each time I checked, he was still on the sofa, but at least he started responding when I asked if he was okay.

"I'm fine. Let me alone. Just let me sleep," he said, but the words were so slurred it had to be from alcohol.

"You've been drinking," I said.

"You've been drinking," he mocked.

I called the pediatrician at 9 a.m. on Sunday morning, and since Joe was a frequent visitor to the clinic, the doctor agreed to phone in a prescription for antibiotics without a hands-on examination. I gave Joe acetaminophen and filled the hot water bottle, which settled him down, and then debated what to do about the church nursery. I had signed up weeks ago to work there for an hour and knew what it was like to be abandoned at the last minute with a room full of active children.

By the time I was dressed, Paul had gotten up and gone to the bathroom, but he looked terrible. There was more red than white in his eyes, and he hadn't shaved. His hair looked like he hads been caught in a windstorm and his clothes were rumpled and slovenly, but he shuffled into the kitchen and poured a cup of coffee. While he drank it, I updated him on Joe's status.

"The doctor is calling in an antibiotic. Are you safe to be alone with him and go get the medicine?" I asked, standing in the kitchen doorway with Matt and Ellen on either side of me and Joe curled on my chest.

"I'm fine. Come on, Joe." He held out his arms, and of course, Joe leaned toward them.

I hesitated, knowing that if Joe stayed home, Paul could get the first dose of antibiotic in him sooner than I would be able to since the pharmacy was less than a mile away.

"Okay." I surrendered Joe, in his fuzzy yellow sleeper pajamas, to his dad. "Please, just make sure you get that medicine."

When I returned home after church, Joe was asleep on Paul's chest, and Paul was just about out, too.

"Did you get his antibiotics?" My heart was on triple speed at the realization it had been a bad decision to depend on Paul just so I could save face with the congregation for an hour.

"What medicine?"

I snatched Joe away from Paul and hustled all the children into the car. The pharmacist knew me well and pulled out the prescription as soon as he saw me standing at the counter. Back at home a few minutes later, I gave Joe a dose of the milky pink liquid and rocked him until he fell back asleep.

Then I told Paul I wanted to speak to him in the bedroom.

"How could you? Joe is sick. I can't believe you would risk your child's health like this."

"Cheryl." He sat down on the bed. "I'm an alcoholic. I have been since college."

In a millisecond, the details of what had previously been our blurry life together cleared. I understood why he had ordered double last call on our first date and drank mine as well as his. The first time I invited him to my house for a meal about a month into our relationship, the small bottle of bourbon I kept in my kitchen cabinet was drained after I came back downstairs from changing my clothes. He had been on the sofa, reading the paper, when I opened the cupboard and saw the nearly empty liquor container.

"Why did you drink the bourbon?" I asked. He snapped the paper shut and gave me a look of total innocence.

"I don't know what you're talking about," he said.

It was crazy—he was the only other adult who had access to the booze, but his convincing response made me question whether it might have spilled or evaporated. In the same way, by the time we were together for six months, I couldn't ignore the way his hands shook.

One time, I laid one of my hands on top of his gently. "Is something wrong?"

"It's an idiopathic tremor," he said. "My doctor told me that was the problem."

He met every challenging question with a glib answer that made me believe he was not an alcoholic. He was a drinker. Somehow that sounded more acceptable until that Sunday morning when he stripped away my carefully constructed shield of denial with one confession.

It was a rough month after that, with tears and accusations and ultimatums. Paul went to a counselor and a physician who helped him detox and I removed all alcohol from our house. I didn't drink when we went to parties where there was alcohol, and I read through the *Twelve Step Book* he brought home from therapy. I watched him closely, wanting to believe he had stopped drinking, just as I wanted to be relieved of being constantly suspicious about his behavior.

The Lewistown crisis passed—or so I thought, never dreaming that again and again I would find empty bottles tucked in random places and pills that looked exactly like sedatives in his pants pockets. Again and again I would confront him, but he would always tell me I was wrong until the evidence accumulated, and he couldn't explain it away.

There was no way to predict the continual discoveries of his drinking, or that he later would add various psychiatric medications to his daily regimen of alcohol. Nor did I understand High Functioning Alcoholism (HFA), a subtype where heavy drinkers manage to live highly productive lives while consuming enormous amounts of alcohol.

By the time these insights dawned, Paul was dead. In Lewistown, I had been in the blissful land of denial or maybe just too busy dealing with our everyday lives to worry about problems that weren't immediate: school permissions and homework, tenure track and teaching evaluations, upkeep of our house and weekly schedules.

Eventually, my anger over Paul's secrets turned into denial that they even existed, and that's how we continued for years. In fact, when he died, I believed he had been in that category of alcoholic labeled "recovered," a notion dispelled at the noisy memorial reception where one of Paul's coworkers stood and proposed a toast. At the time, I was talking to someone else, so it seemed like a mistake.

"Here's to Paul. Boy, he could really get going after a few drinks," the man said, holding up a wine glass, "I'll never forget him taking on a senior partner."

It couldn't be true. Paul always told me it was difficult for him to go to work-related activities involving alcohol because he was often the only person who wasn't drinking.

"You know I can't be around booze," he would explain when he arrived home a few hours after the event (usually a mandatory meeting) started.

I followed up on the coworker's comment the following week by asking Sue, the secretary who had worked with Paul for decades, if he had been drinking right before he died. We were at lunch and my question made her look up from her plate of food. For a moment, her blue eyes held mine and her face tensed.

"Cheryl, he never stopped. We all knew it; in fact, a memo circulated asking 'people' to stop putting beer cans in the freezer for a quick chill before happy hour. Paul was always the one who did it." She relaxed and laughed. "Of course, they would explode all over because he would forget they were there."

Although I nodded at her and attempted a smile, I had seen Paul do the same thing at home, pretending the beer was for me or a guest. After he died, I cleaned out his suits before donating them and found anti-anxiety pills in many of the pockets, I still couldn't think of him as an addict.

Guilt surged through me as we chugged away from Lewistown, even though I knew Paul made the choices that led to substance abuse long before he met me. Would I have been able to curb his addiction? And what might have been different if he lived and died later from the ominous mass that the ER X-rays identified on his kidney? Would he have come clean about his drinking, sparing me the shocking discoveries that felt so much like betrayal?

Those questions were like so many of the "if-onlys" I had heard other family members who lost loved ones to tragic accidents repeat over the years.

"If only he had stayed home that night, he wouldn't have crashed the car."

"If only she had taken better care of herself, she wouldn't have gotten sick."

Even parents whose young children had died of terminal diseases talked about what they might have overlooked that could have led to a cure. On the first leg of my train trip, it felt like I was in the magical land of "if-only" again, hurtling west on a train.

altoona
the daily pennsylvanian

Before children, before booze, and before marriage, I had a reliable solution for dealing with problems: I ran away. In the three years after graduating from nursing school, I had relocated seven times and gone through an equal number of jobs.

"You know, you seem like a strong candidate for this position, but you've moved around a lot," the interviewer at my first academic job noted, scanning the three pages of my resume. "Was something going on?"

Usually, it was a failed romance or disappointing workplace that led to my search for a new and better home. My worldly belongings would fit in my orange Datsun B-210, and everyone was hiring nurses in those days, so it was easy to hop from man to man and hospital to hospital. Although some of the moves didn't work out—like when I discovered a month after relocating that a Pennsylvania nursing license wasn't valid in New York—it was exciting to start over again and again.

After Paul died, I debated using that strategy again, perhaps relocating to Florida where Susan and some remote family members lived, concluding that I couldn't leave my daughter, who was still in Hershey, or Joe and his family. That's what I told myself, but really, I was short on energy. As a new widow, there just wasn't enough motivation in me to go looking for a new job and new home.

When I told my sister, Beth, that it felt like I was living in a house full of painful memories, she understood. My place had been the center of family gatherings over the holidays every year since we bought it. An hour later, she arrived at my door with a bundle of sage in one hand.

"This is to get rid of bad spirits," she said, lighting it.

I followed her through the house, watching as she wafted sage smoke throughout, with a special concentration on the areas Paul favored: the far corner of the sofa, his computer desk, and the books on the family room shelf. It was touching to see how seriously she took her efforts, even though nothing changed because of them.

Or maybe something did, because not long after she visited, I booked a different kind of journey than the ones I had taken before. I might not have been able to pack up all my belongings and move, but I could pack one suitcase and ride the train.

Don, a travel agent at AAA, had organized previous vacations for me. Hours after coming up with the idea, I was in his office.

"I want to start in Harrisburg and go as far west as possible by train," I told him.

"How long? Northern or Southern route?" he asked, his fingers already tapping out information on the special computer screen that told him what was available.

"Out by the northern route and back by the southern? I'd love to see New Orleans."

Without pausing, he grimaced and shook his head. "No can do. Since Katrina that's a tourist hot spot—try me next year."

I waited while he went to retrieve a sheaf of papers from the printer. "You ever seen the Horseshoe Curve, outside Altoona?" He handed me a copy of the printout and inserted the other in a manila folder.

I shook my head. "Is it scary?"

"Some people think it's an adventure. Good way to start a trip."

"I've heard of it, but this'll be my first train trip west. Usually I go east to Philadelphia or New York."

"No kidding?" He paused, the stapler still in his hand. "Well, it's always good to explore new places, and aren't you an author? Maybe you'll get some material for a new book."

As I drove the short distance to my house with the thick packet of tickets on my car's front seat, I found myself thinking—wishing—that there might be a memoir-worthy epiphany awaiting me—maybe in Montana, a state I'd never visited, or outside of Portland, Oregon, another area on my "to see" list. Then I would close the chapter on my year of disaster and feel like I was finally moving forward.

Really? There it was again, the cynical voice inside my head.

You think one train trip is going to jumpstart a life that's been going in reverse for the past year?

Why not? I countered. A change of scenery and tempo might be just what I needed to reason out an answer to the question that had been tick-tocking through my brain since the day I left my husband's lifeless body at the hospital and went home: What happened? How could he fall so hard on the bottom steps of a stairway that he died almost instantly?

I had asked Sue to request Paul's medical records for me but couldn't find any clues in the Xeroxed pages. Late one night, I contacted the resident whose signature was scrawled across the discharge summary.

"I just found out that my husband was actively drinking before he died—he had problems in the past," I said. "I don't want you to think I was dishonest with the information I gave you."

"I didn't think that at all, but he did have a lot of alcohol on board that morning when he got here," the resident said.

As soon as I hung up, I took out the records, already fringed with my annotated Post-It notes. On the section devoted to lab results, there was a page with only one line printed across the top, easily overlooked. The morning he fell and died, Paul's Blood Alcohol Concentration (BAC) at 6:30 a.m. had been .30. The usual cutoff for drunk driving is .08, while .30 leads to "acute confusion and even coma."

How could that be? When I had pressed my mouth to his to do CPR that morning, there was no taste of alcohol; I would have noticed. His empty coffee cup had been long washed, but surely the smell would have been obvious.

The lack of an answer I could believe led me to make an appointment with Kate, a therapist who had treated us both as a couple and individually, for several years. I knew Paul had seen her frequently throughout the year before his death and thought she might be able to provide some insights.

As soon as I sat down in her office, I said, "Was Paul still drinking around the time when he died?"

She didn't look away or blink. "You were going away on a work-related trip, and he thought he could go into rehab and pull it off without telling you. He was afraid you would leave him if you found out this time."

If she had thrown her cup of coffee on me, it wouldn't have shocked more. The weekend of his blackout in Lewistown had been wrenching, but also hopeful. Then, I believed I could do something to help him—in fact that's what I devoted myself to doing.

I was a good nurse, and I taught students how to be good nurses, but with Paul, none of my empathy or skill or training had worked. That reality hit me hard after he was dead.

He wasn't a "recovering alcoholic" who avoided social functions involving booze—he openly embraced them so he could drink for a few hours and then come home and tell me he hadn't been able to tolerate the environment. He wasn't using medications carefully and as prescribed—he went to different doctors, stockpiled prescriptions, and littered pills on the floor where small children or pets might find them. His hands didn't shake from a benign tremor, and empty bottles didn't mysteriously appear in our house or cars. He was a hard-core drinker who had never changed, just as Sue had told me.

What other things had he deceived me about for the better part of the years we spent together? It was unbearable to consider.

———

The Altoona train stop brought up other memories I had buried. My grandparents lived in a tiny town near there, and when my parents would make their biannual pilgrimage to visit, we sometimes went to Altoona, the closest "city" where shopping was available. Having grown up near Binghamton, New York, in its heyday, I was surprised by the cracked streets and abandoned buildings that constituted a city in Pennsylvania, sure I would never want to live in such a backward state. Somehow, that's exactly what happened: Lancaster, Philadelphia, State College, Harrisburg, Lewistown, and Hershey were spots on the Pennsylvania map that ended up connecting my family, career, and personal life in adulthood.

My grandparents were a big influence on my life. As the first grandchild, I was the beneficiary of lots of affection both in the form of candy and sweets (over my mother's protests) and the spotlight of their adoring attention. Then, in the fifth grade, I went to stay with them for a week and experienced abuse at the hands of my grandfather. It was confusing, because I loved him and had always felt special when he singled me out for affection, but then he changed behavior and did things that hurt me.

I didn't speak about what happened until I was married to Paul. My parents refused to believe me, especially when my brother shared an article with them on "False Memories," suggesting he didn't believe me either.

It's taken me a long time to recognize how I was conditioned early on to question the truth of my recollections and feelings. My grandfather acted one way when other people were around and differently when it was just him and me, but for years I didn't tell anyone because that seemed just too unlikely to be true. He was my grandfather. I loved him. Later, when Paul turned out to be a person who said one thing and did another, I was already primed on how to respond.

———

There was a stir of excitement in the rail car of The Daily Pennsylvanian as we approached "The Curve." If Lee was really a consultant to the military and loved the train as much as he suggested, he should know about some of the intrigue surrounding the spot. I decided to test my theory.

"Oh wow." I leaned in his direction to look out the window. "I think we're coming up to the Horseshoe Curve. Do you know about it?"

Lee's expression barely changed. "It's a tourist trap. Not that big of a deal."

For western Pennsylvanians, the Horseshoe Curve, constructed over a three-year period beginning in 1850, is a big deal. Added to the National Register of Historic Places because of an engineering miracle that created an incline which rises nine degrees every 100 feet, it was a tourist favorite because passengers got a view of the end of the train as they traveled, and it seemed to be going in the opposite direction.

There are other bits of train history that relate to Altoona. During World War II, the Germans launched "Operation Pastorius," which involved recruiting eight German Americans and training them to sabotage the United States through terrorist actions. The Horseshoe Curve was one of the sites targeted for bombing since it was a crucial hub for the railroad and strategically close to train repair shops in Altoona.

The eight Germans were divided into contingents, with two men delivered to Long Island via submarine and nearly captured by the Coast Guard. Another six landed in Florida.

The two men delivered to the north decided to defect, but when they called the FBI, no one believed their story. It took a personal visit with a briefcase full of cash to convince Herbert Hoover to dispatch agents to Florida, where the others were soon arrested, judged at a military tribunal, and quickly executed via the electric chair. The northerner defectors went to prison for a long time, and thereafter, the Horseshoe Curve had an armed guard around-the-clock.

Paul, a World War II buff, would have searched the library for more information about that event. Before long, his brain would have been full of facts and anecdotes, for future use or entertainment.

"You know they found Americans who spoke perfect German, Cheryl," is the kind of thing he would have told me, launching into other stories of spies and intrigue.

I tried to snap a picture through the window Lee partially blocked, but we were already around the curve and headed toward Johnstown for a scheduled stop. If anyone asked me whether the ride had been scary, I would have to say the videos I later watched online were more impressive than the actual experience, but that was okay. At that point, there was already more than enough drama in my life.

johnstown
the daily pennsylvanian

The conductor called out to announce a true rest stop in Johnstown (as opposed to a flag stop where passengers can only exit or enter), the first one of the trip. I joined the people who were filing out, grateful for the opportunity to stretch my legs and stand on a platform that wasn't vibrating or rocking back and forth. The man who had been trapped in place by his loquacious seatmate behind me bee-lined toward a woman and girl who were standing together, clearly waiting for him.

"What the heck?" the woman said, rolling her eyes and patting him on the shoulder.

"Daddy, that man sitting next to you really talks a lot," his daughter said. She looked about the age of my five-year-old granddaughter.

"Shhh," her mother cautioned, but Lee and I were the only ones standing near enough to hear.

Without his captive audience, the chatty fellow in the turban wandered out, searching around the platform for another listener, but everyone who had been within hearing radius turned their backs on him. He sighted Lee and me and closed in.

"Do you know how truly wonderful God is?" he asked us.

Lee held up his hands, palms out, as if to shove the man away, "I'm an atheist, so don't even bother."

Was there more to that brief encounter than I realized at the time? Was the man giving Lee a hidden message, or was Lee signaling a warning that sent the man scurrying away? Given my misunderstanding of my own husband's inner struggles, I had very low confidence in my observational skills by then, but something still nagged at me about Lee. He was traveling without luggage, claiming his wife was meeting him in Pittsburgh, which meant he had come all the way from Boston with nothing more than the clothes he wore—not even a cellphone. That in addition to his covert glances toward the seat behind us and semi-hostile behavior on the platform were surely grounds for suspicion.

Right. You're great at figuring people out, my inner voice said. *Don't forget about your major misstep with Jack, too.*

Jack. My first and perhaps wildest ever romance after Paul's death was one more thing that had turned out badly in my first year of widowhood. Had things gone differently, Jack might be standing next to me on the train platform, face lifted to the late afternoon sun.

"I think I'm going to go with you," he said when he saw my *Amtrak Vacations* magazine with the cross-country route high-lighted in yellow. At that point, our relationship was an emotional equivalent of the Horseshoe Curve, inching uphill one glorious moment and then seeming to slide backwards the next.

"Do you want the top or the bottom?" I showed him a diagram of the tiny sleeping compartment in the train catalogue and his eyebrows met in a frown. He didn't mention joining me again, but it didn't matter anyway since he unexpectedly broke up with me a few days later.

I met Jack as my first winter without Paul approached and leaves drifted off the trees like slow tears. It seemed possible I might die of sorrow, since I was still losing weight and couldn't explain why even a morsel of nourishment felt like an unwanted attempt to keep on living. Frustrated, my family doctor referred me to a gastrointestinal specialist to explore why I could not eat, and her diagnosis was spot on: I had the anorexia of grief.

"Have you thought about trying to meet someone?" my good friend, Kathy, asked one day when we met for lunch. She was my mentor in widowhood, a woman whose husband had died of a fast-acting form of cancer before their children were grown and out of the house. Now, she was remarried and on the other side of grief, but the memory of her dissolving into tears during a planning meeting to plan for my Camp Ophelia program has always stayed with me.

"It would take too much energy," I told her, although I had wondered about the same thing.

I couldn't stand the thought of trolling bars to find a man like I did in my younger years, especially when the single women I knew were uniformly pessimistic about meeting men.

"It's a jungle out there," said one divorcee, who hadn't dated since meeting her ex-husband thirty years prior.

"I guess I'm back on the prowl again," said another middle-ager, more familiar with the online scene. "I'm going to try a different app this time. Maybe eHarmony—I hear they attract a more mellow crowd."

"They ask for your measurements. It's unbelievable," yet another, now married, had cautioned.

To me, scrolling through profiles and ruling out people it might otherwise take months to reject had seemed efficient and practical when I was single and there was no reason for me to need such help. As the hours I spent alone in my bedroom grew longer, I wondered what it would be like to just look at a dating site. One night I picked one randomly and logged on. An hour later, all I could think of was Paul—I missed him more than ever. He had been my partner for over half of my adult life, so being single was unnatural, but the kind of intimacy we shared didn't seem readily available online.

There also seemed to be a stigma to using online dating sites once you reached a "mature" age. The era and family I grew up in was one where you waited to be asked out. In the years before marriage, I had enjoyed many relationships, but none overtly initiated by me, so looking for a potential match on the Internet felt like asking a man out. Theoretically acceptable, but a big step outside my comfort zone.

Then there was the discovery that men who were up to ten years older than me seemed to gravitate into one of three groups. The Bikers, adult boys who stood beside their motorcycles or straddled the saddle looked ready to head off the second after the picture was taken. The Posers included pictures of themselves in various types of clothing, often bare-chested. The Parentals, a category I gravitated towards, were guys who loved their animals and grandchildren.

I checked out the female profiles out of curiosity. There weren't many women my age or with the body of a person who had given birth, worked hard, and lived past middle age. Those who were brave enough to post had faces that bore traces of the joys and sorrows they had experienced and hair with the grey highlighted out, just like mine. How could I/we compete with younger, bikini-clad girls who didn't mind being with the same "older men" we might pursue?

I returned to the male side of the service and decided to create a profile that was different. Instead of spelling out the details of my demographics, I composed an admittedly silly rhyme poem and posted a headshot of me in business attire. It was calculated to instantly weed out men in search of a babe to ride behind them on their superbike.

Jack contacted me within days, sending an equally light ditty back. The other responses were mostly one word ("Hi" or "Hey") or from men who suggested we "meet up." A few were from distant locations and other countries; one even proposed marriage. There was a note in very bad English that extolled my "sexiness picture" and a different one that was downright disturbing.

I answered Jack's poem with one of my own. He returned yet another, but suggested we knew each other well enough to forego the rhymes and talk normally by phone. I agreed to do away with the creativity but still wanted to stick with emailing to protect my personal information.

Figuring out the rules of Internet dating was confusing. It seemed there might not be any—it was okay to ask a woman for her picture in a bathing suit and ready to hook up in real time after one email if the virtual chemistry felt right. That's what Jack wanted to do after our series of playful exchanges, but I wasn't ready for a date. I told him I wanted to get to know each other first, and he seemed content to do a little more electronic correspondence.

It wasn't long before I was checking my email hourly; the world brightened when some Jack banter came my way. Eventually, I gave him my regular email address, which contained my name, and he did the same. We promptly Googled each other, and our relationship went to a new level of interest as I discovered that he was an attorney who probably knew Paul. He was curious to learn that I was a professor in the College of Medicine. There were more questions around these discoveries, and finally, I relented and gave him my phone number so we could talk in real time. The sound of his voice on the first call made my stomach flutter in a way I vaguely remembered.

One week later, we met for a drink at a nice restaurant halfway between our locations. When I came in and saw him sitting at the bar, he looked much like his profile picture: not especially handsome but strangely intriguing. As soon as I perched on the high seat next to him, he smiled and leaned toward me.

"Dr. Dellasega. Nice to meet you," he said, and then gestured for the bartender to bring me a drink.

We talked for two hours, and when we went to the parking lot to go our separate ways, he asked if he could kiss me goodnight. I offered my cheek and got the sexiest non-mouth kiss of my life. I still had the anguished angular look of a woman in grief, so the idea that any man might find me attractive was enough to send me sailing home in an ether of alcohol-induced happiness.

Like me, Jack had been married before. In the weeks that followed, I learned about his past and what he hoped for in the future. He had two adult children he adored who lived on either side of the country. His house was filled with books, photographs he took and framed, and trophies from his athletic competitions. Although he was a successful attorney, he wanted to do more—maybe write a book, return to school, or backpack across Europe.

Within a month of our first date, Jack said that he loved me and that he knew I loved him too. He handwrote a beautiful poem— more elegant than our emailed ones—on expensive paper and left it on my front porch. He sent flowers to the main hospital desk, so that everyone I worked with saw me carrying a bouquet back to my office with a goofy grin on my face. That's when I began to enjoy eating again because if Jack didn't cook, we ate in out-of-the-way places with food he knew would be good.

"Do you love me yet?" Jack would ask each time we were together.

"I'm very fond of you," I would say.

I rotated "fond" with having "great affection" for him, "caring deeply," and being "so grateful that we met." By the time we were spending every spare minute together, I began to think I might actually love him. Like Paul, he had a job which required him to convince people to believe what he said, whether it was true or not. Unlike Paul, he was full of self-assurance and that kind of easy sexiness some men seem to wear like aftershave.

Although we became "a couple," spending weekends and sometimes weeknights together and texting constantly the rest of the time, I refused Jack's pressure to post something about our status, which felt like a public betrayal of Paul. New to the world of Facebook, I didn't realize there were many meanings to the status of "in a relationship" or why it seemed so important to Jack.

When his daughter came home from college for the December holidays, I couldn't wait to meet her. When Jack talked about Soni (short for Sonya), the lines of his face turned soft, and a faraway look came into his eyes. She was bright, attractive, and...she was Jack's daughter.

For the first time in my history of connecting with young women, things didn't go well. Soni wasn't especially interested in getting to know me, and suddenly, Jack's emails and phone calls were all about her and the fun things they were doing together. I only saw him when Soni had plans that didn't include him.

After churning the situation over during a few sleepless nights, I shrugged it off. Soni had Jack to herself for many years and was used to getting all his attention. Although she went to school a short distance away, he didn't get to see her that often and justifiably wanted to be with her, so I kept busy babysitting and catching up with the friends I had begun to ignore because I was busy with Jack.

"Don't ever ask me to choose you over my daughter," he said, when I suggested he was spending a lot of time with her.

I frowned at him. "That's like comparing apples and oranges. You can't have a relationship with your children that's anything like a relationship with a lover."

"Cheryl, I'm just telling you, if you ever put me in the position of picking, I will always go with her." The way he spoke felt almost like a challenge I couldn't imagine making.

His behavior was almost as weird as his instantaneous love, but who was I to object? My son and daughter-in-law were still living with me, and my Saturday nights were often spent with my granddaughter. If I was needed for childcare during a time I had scheduled with Jack, I changed my plans and went home—was that putting him in second place?

When Soni returned to college, we picked up as if nothing had happened. Sometimes, as we headed for the exit of a bar or turned a street corner, Jack would grab me and flatten me against the nearest wall to make out. Once, he pulled me into the men's bathroom of a classy restaurant for a long passionate kiss. Those things made our relationship soar, but then, just as surely, it would crash and burn for unpredictable reasons. The mention of another man would set him off, which made it hard to talk about my day since my coworkers at the time were 90% male. I had to start censoring what I would share with him and avoided taking him any place where I might encounter a male coworker or friend.

Every so often, without warning, he would get angry and tell me we were finished. There were times when I inadvertently did something that offended him, leading to a negative reaction, but there were also times when I was completely clueless about why he temporarily broke off contact.

My daughter-in-law looked at me sideways while cooking dinner one night after my second faux break up with Jack.

"You know, I don't think he's very good for you," she said, but I brushed my tears away as soon as he called and promptly left the house to meet him at one of our favorite hangouts so we could patch things up.

My disagreements with Paul had been quiet. Perhaps, over the years, we wore each other out and settled into a passive silence instead of fury. Jack, on the other hand, was easily incited, and as our relationship progressed, our battles turned furious and cruel. I discovered a vitriolic side of myself that I hated.

The end came when Soni's plans for the summer changed at the last minute. Jack had initially thought she would be doing a work/study program far away and had already suggested we spend the entire time together, traveling and having fun.

"No, no, it's okay, of course I want you home," he said the morning she called with the news that her plan had fallen through and she would be at his place within days, but for at least a second after he hung up, there was a crestfallen look on his face. Soon enough, though, she arrived home and it was a repeat of the holidays.

The weekend of our grand finale was preceded by several days of conflict. One morning we were on our way to a farmer's market when Soni called, perhaps out of loneliness. I encouraged Jack to go and be with her, but not without wondering what the future held for us. Just after claiming he wanted to go on the Amtrak trip with me, Jack invited me to go to the circus with Soni and him, a tradition they had enjoyed since her childhood. On the way to the show, they chuckled about shared memories and made inside jokes I couldn't appreciate and wasn't told.

After taking our seats, with Jack in the middle, the National Anthem was announced. Of the three of us, I was the only one to stand up.

"Cheryl, you don't have to stand up," Jack said in a loud "bad child" voice. He and Soni exchanged a look that suggested she shared his opinion.

As the mother of a military child, I didn't hesitate. "I want to stand up."

The people seated around us turned to watch, as if anticipating more conflict. Instead, Jack and Soni put their heads together, said something too low for me to hear and then laughed. That kind of behavior continued for the rest of the show.

The next day, I waited for him to call. Usually, I would hear from him after I came home from church, but it was early evening when my cellphone finally lit up.

"What a day," he said. "We went grocery shopping, then stopped for coffee and ended up at the bookstore. I'm exhausted, but I could meet you for a drink if you want."

"Oh, that's okay. I'm going to the art festival downtown, so don't worry about it."

There was silence. "Who are you going with?"

"A friend," I said.

"Who is he?" Even with the phone away from my ear, I could hear his voice. "You planned this without telling me? That's it, Cheryl."

He hung up and refused to pick up when I called back. After two days of no contact, I emailed to tell Jack I had stopped at his house to try and retrieve my only pair of eyeglasses, but no one was home, so could he please return them? His phone call was immediate.

"If you ever come on my street again, I will call the police," he said.

"Are you kidding? All I want is my glasses. I need them."

"I will return all your things. Do not come on my property."

This was not going to turn into another nasty battle that we would eventually admit was stupid: Jack had crossed a line. Maybe that line wouldn't have been so apparent at another time in my life, but just then my daughter was in a particularly bad spot and my tolerance for bad behavior was strained.

"Do it soon," I said, and hung up the phone before I lost control. What exactly did he think I was going to do to his run-down "property"?

Between Jack's jealousy and moodiness, and my depression and neediness, our relationship had probably been destined to fail, but to this day we both remember a man who sat behind us on an air flight from Arizona to Philadelphia. Passengers were lining up in the aisle to exit the plane when this gentleman leaned forward.

He said, "I wish I had what you two have. Take care of it—it's precious."

It was a prickly relationship. In some ways, Jack will always be the man who saved my life and then broke my heart—but although I flirted with the idea of resuming our relationship when he suggested it several times in the years that followed, I just stopped caring. I walked out of his life ten pounds heavier and soon after boarded a train that would take me as far away from him and all my other problems as possible.

latrobe
the daily pennsylvanian

Outside the window, the Pennsylvania landscape looked like a rippling ribbon of green grass, brown earth, and clear blue sky, spooling out as we traveled. We were in an area the *Amtrak America* magazine didn't feature; there were no Amish buggies, curling rivers, or urban skylines, just one miniature rural town after another. One of those was Labrobe, population 8000, listed on the Amtrak website as a Great American (Train) Station, despite its size.

In the midst of rolling farmland and little else, Latrobe was nonetheless famous for Rolling Rock beer, which got its start in a brewery there. The little green cans had always been somewhat of a joke because of its supposedly low alcohol content, but that was back in my fraternity party days, when I wasn't paying for my drinks and couldn't have distinguished between a Sierra Nevada and a Pabst Blue Ribbon. The boys and the music and the possibilities of the evening were what my best friend, Susan, and I cared about.

She and I were unlikely School of Nursing students. Our class had a fair contingent of local Mennonites bound for mission service, one male, and one African American (the latter two a first), but the rest of our peers came from nearby areas in Pennsylvania. Most of them cleared out of the dormitory on weekends, leaving Susan and me to entertain ourselves—and we did.

My first year after graduating high school at age seventeen was a time when it felt like my life was finally on the fast forward I wanted: plenty of boys, two different roommates, a stream of friends, and learning new things. Freed from my parents' heavy oversight, I could finally go where I wanted, as long as I made the mandatory curfew. It was also when I took my first train trip, which seemed incredibly glamorous even though it was short.

My memory isn't clear on how it happened, but on the morning of that first trip that would take me partway home, I was outside my dormitory before realizing my blue pleather suitcase was much too heavy to carry to the train station a half mile away. It was too late to try and find a ride, so through a combination of desperation and physical fitness, I discovered that if I swung the bag forward with one hand, took a running giant step, and then transferred it to the other, some law of physics made forward progress possible. Fueled by anxiety and my slow run, I made it just on time.

That adventure didn't cure me of over-packing, but it did spark a love of train riding. Neither the rundown station nor the train car's pungent smells were especially appealing but the adventure within an adventure was. As we flew over the tracks toward what was, to me, an unknown and therefore exciting destination, I eavesdropped on passengers who were talking about their travel, disciplining their children, or joking with the conductor.

I would discover that train connections are surprisingly intimate but brief. When we arrived at our destinations, people would go their separate ways, strangers again, much like Lee and I were likely to do. At the same time, all those years ago, seeing the world pass by my window in a blur hooked me, and from that day forward I would travel by train whenever it was an option.

———

Since Johnstown, Lee continued to extract information from me about my past. In turn, he revealed that he and his ex-wife, with whom he was reconciling, planned to connect in Pittsburgh and catch a plane to Atlanta where their first grandchild had arrived days earlier.

He could have flown and had a quicker and perhaps more comfortable trip, but he explained he was a railfan and, like me, loved to travel that way. (A railfan is a reasonable enthusiast, unlike foamers, who take their emotions to extremes.) Looking back, it sounds even more improbable than it did when it happened. A military consultant without at least a briefcase to see him through a long journey? A man meeting up with his divorced wife to go and visit his daughter? A seatmate whose eyes kept shifting in the direction of the loquacious Pakistani?

"So, are you happily married?" He didn't look at me when he asked the most personal of his questions, but probably sensed how off guard he caught me.

"I was. My husband died a year ago."

Widow. Why can't you just say it? Now you'll just get caught up in explaining a painful situation. The mental dialogue of my mean voice didn't help in the uncomfortable silence that followed.

"What happened? You're pretty young to be a widow."

In another setting, I might have snapped back, "Death doesn't discriminate," or, "That's too personal," but I was on a train where the normal mores of conversation got suspended. I launched into the story I had repeated so many times it was like a favorite song from the 1970s; each word, rhythm, and pause was ingrained in my mind.

In the early post-death days, it had been important to include each detail of the chronology when sharing the description: our last meal together, the Christmas sweatshirt and jeans I grabbed to wear to the hospital in early June, Lacey wandering outside and through the neighborhood after I left the front door open for the ambulance crew, and so much more. One year later, I had a condensed version, but not a better way to tell it.

"My husband was 56 years old, and in pretty good health. He was going down to the basement to get a shirt for work one morning and fell on the bottom steps and that was it. We got to the hospital quickly, but he had such a massive bleed in his brain that any kind of normal life was impossible, even with surgery."

"That's rough," he said, his gray eyes meeting mine. For a second, I felt the tug on my throat that usually signaled tears.

"We were together for 28 years," I said, looking away. "Funny how you don't appreciate something like that when it's actually happening."

"What was he like?" Lee acted as if we were old friends catching up on the years that had elapsed since we last spoke. I'm not sure what he wanted to know, but I sketched out Paul: wicked funny, super smart, a dad, a son, and a husband. Then I was done sharing my past with him.

"I'm going to stretch a bit," I said, before he could ask about my sex life.

On the train you can actually move around, so I walked the

55

length of the car and hit the release buttons on the doors that connected each car to the next. On TV and in the movies, it's more glamorous and treacherous to go from car to car; on a real passenger train there aren't many opportunities to hang off the side or climb up to the top.

The next car was a carbon copy of mine; people were working, conversing, or sleeping, but no one looked like Lee: solitary and without distraction, gazing out the window as if in a trance. I ducked into one of the bathrooms farther away from my seat and splashed some water on my face.

In the scratched mirror, my blurred image looked even sadder than I felt at that moment. If Paul was alive, he would be on this trip with me; instead I was trapped in the only seat available, next to a person who could be a mass murderer or CIA operative.

Keep your guard up with that Lee and just get to Pittsburgh. Once you're there, you can grab the first train back to Harrisburg and consider this a lesson learned, my inner critic suggested.

It had been an exhausting day for someone who usually counted time and regularly collapsed in the bedroom as part of her daily routine. Figuring out what supplies I would need for the trip and then packing them all up, saying goodbye to Lacey, who didn't realize I was putting a country between me and her, giving my granddaughter a farewell hug, and then navigating the train station had taken a lot of my precious energy. Fending Lee's verbal parries while drowning out the constant chatter of the man behind us had tipped me into overload.

As I made my way down the aisle holding on to the backs of seats on either side of me, it felt like we were all on a rocket hurtling into the frontier of space instead of clacking over railroad tracks millions of others had used to get to a familiar destination. At least we would soon be in Pittsburgh, the first leg of my trip would be over, and we were right on schedule—something I expected. A fire or electrical failure might lead to hours of delay on Amtrak, and once, a complete cancellation occurred after a suicidal person jumped onto the tracks, but short delays were rare.

When I dropped back into my seat, the Pakistani man was still talking, but Lee seemed to be dozing. Looking past him, I felt guilty for having talked to an attractive stranger so candidly about

Paul. Of course, I hadn't told him how I didn't push Paul for an explanation when he tripped over the lightweight love seat moments before he went down the fatal stairs, or that he had dropped and broken a plate the night before as he carried his pizza to the table for dinner. I didn't mention his heart-wrenching recitation of Ernest Thayer's famous poem "Casey at the Bat" which he felt captured his situation at work.

"Are you sure you're okay?" I had asked at what would turn out to be our last dinner. The subtext of that question was always, "Are you drinking?"

Paul had an interesting face that never changed. If he was happy, there might be fewer lines on his forehead, and if he was depressed, his features might sag a bit, but that night there had been an aura of despair around him—one that I sensed rather than saw.

"I realized today that I just can't keep up. I've always been the 'go-to' guy who could answer any question or figure out an angle to any case, but I see these young lawyers building their careers and I can't do it anymore."

"Retire," I said, as I always did when he seemed especially anxious about the job he loved more than he disliked.

"What would I do? Be a teacher? How would we pay for health insurance?"

It was a standing joke between us. He thought being an educator would be an easy job, especially since he had such a passion for world history. Having been in the classroom with students only slightly removed from their high school years, I thought he might find teaching just as challenging as practicing law, but we still went back and forth about it in a bantering way. That night there was something different about his worry, and he didn't follow the familiar script.

I said, "Think about doing something different. You know I'll support you."

"We need to save money. Who knows what's ahead?" He looked down at Lacey, who was by his feet in the hopes of being fed a scrap or two. "No. I'm stuck for now." Then, after another few seconds, he cited the last stanza of the poem while staring out the window, as if there was something only he could see.

"Oh, somewhere in this favored land, the sun is shining bright/

The band is playing somewhere, and somewhere hearts are light,/
And somewhere men are laughing, and somewhere children shout/
But there is no joy in Mudville—mighty Casey has struck out."

pittsburg
the capitol limited

From the slice of train window I could see beyond Lee's profile, farmland had broken into rougher terrain bordered by mountains, and then, gradually, housing developments appeared, and we entered the city borders. I watched the window like I might a chain of mindless commercials on prime-time television, relieved that finally, my seatmate did not turn to me and resume his questioning.

"Ladies and gentlemen, we are now approaching our final stop," the conductor said over the public announcement system. "Now arriving in Pittsburgh. Please be careful as you go from the train to the platform. Pittsburgh, now arriving in Pittsburgh."

The conductor was a good one, making sure we knew where we were as the train rumbled into the station. More than once, I had nearly missed my home train stop in tiny Elizabethtown because so few people got off there. If I failed to watch for our approach, I could be sitting with my laptop on and my suitcase far away from the exit doors when we screeched to a halt.

One time, a colleague from New York City traveled by train to give a talk at Hershey. She phoned me ahead of time to ask for instructions.

"Should I call a taxi when I get to Elizabethtown?"

"No, you should get ready to jump when the train slows," I told her with a laugh. "And then I'll be there to pick you up."

Not true in Pittsburgh, a major train station. As we eased to a stop, unlike the dramatic arrival in Harrisburg, people grabbed their bags and shuffled forward in the aisle, eager to de-board.

"Good luck with your travels. I'll be looking for your book on the bestseller list." Lee winked and stepped out into the aisle. The turbaned man was just ahead of him, and without further pause, Lee headed after him toward the exit.

We hadn't exchanged email addresses or any other contact information, so I wasn't likely to see him again. Still, should some tragedy happen during the trip leading my photograph to appear on the "Missing Persons" segment of evening television, there was a comfort in knowing Lee would be able to identify me.

I had a long layover in Pittsburgh so there was no rush, but for some reason I felt it important to make my way to the train station's waiting room where I found the atmosphere of a New Year's party without the alcohol. People were packed into every seat and spilling out from the standing spaces, so the only way I could sit was by crouching on the edge of my suitcase. It wasn't long before my back cramped, and I was forced to stand up. My flip flops stuck to the floor when I shifted positions, and my lumbar spine was beginning to revolt from the stress of prolonged sitting alternated with the toting of heavy baggage.

In the center of the room, an Amish family opened an aluminum cooler the size of a steamer trunk and a bonneted woman began doling out food to the group of black clad people around her. Quickly, they accepted bottles of creamy milk and slices of thick bread that was sure to be homemade, which made me realize a hasty breakfast had been my last meal. Thanks to Jack, my body had grown used to being fed at regular intervals and now I was starved.

With the exception of New York City, I hadn't found a train station that offered more than vending machine meals, but at the end of a long day without food, even peanut butter crackers and chocolate milk was an appealing dinner. As the Amish group settled in to enjoy their food, each bite they took made my hunger grow.

I went back out into the long hallway and found a soda machine in working order, but my crumpled dollar bill was rejected again and again. There was a man in a non-train uniform behind the ticket counter; when I asked if there was a place in the station to get any kind of food, he said, "Nope," in the way someone who fielded the question a lot would.

Standing in front of him with my stomach clenched in hunger and my brain drained by Lee, I sagged in defeat. This trip really was a colossal mistake. If there was a train leaving to go back home just then, I would have climbed on it instantly, bound for my bed and Lacey, but the Harrisburg route was closed until the next day.

In a post-9/11/01 era, there were no lockers to store suitcases, so once more, I took a deep breath and gathered up my belongings.

According to the ticket guy, there was a hotel a block away that *might* have a restaurant inside.

It was 8:30 P.M. and I knew nothing about the geography of the neighborhood around Union Station. Widows (myself included), are often stripped of their confidence and willingness to venture beyond the known when they become suddenly single. Having interviewed and counseled many who lost their partners to death, I knew that for the most part, men could be in this world alone without worrying that they will be sexually accosted or harassed. Women cannot.

I was still ambivalent about continuing my trip, which is typical for those who grieve. Part of you wants to move on to a "new" life without the person you lost, and yet to do so can feel like disrespect or negation of an important relationship.

After fifteen minutes of internal debate, I mustered up my courage and lumbered outside the station, trailing my aged, wheeled suitcase behind me. If Paul was alive, he might be by my side or on the cellphone, talking me through the long walk ahead, but of course there was no Paul or anyone else to call.

A fine mist of rain looked like static in the air, and no one was visible on the poorly lit streets, but I continued in the direction of a block where there might be a restaurant, determined to carry out my search for food and a possible beverage. I was beginning to feel shaky and the idea of an ice-cold beer, the ultimate refreshment at the end of a long day, was suddenly enticing. Although alcohol had never been a particular vice of mine, a frosty Coors Light was my favorite drink in the summer, when nothing else seemed to satisfy my thirst in quite the same way.

What *had* become a vice were pills. The time since Paul's death could be titled, "My Year of Living Chemically." I had steadily accumulated prescriptions for the same medicines I prescribed when working as a nurse practitioner for patients who were anxious, depressed, in pain, or sleeping poorly. Some of them were identical to the pills I discovered in Paul's drawers and clothing after he died.

Increasingly, I made sure I had a supply of my rainbow assortment of psychoactive drugs when I left home. Yes, they were all legal and dispensed by my physicians, but I knew what could happen and took care to rotate my use of them so my body wouldn't come to depend on any one substance. They wouldn't be any help to me now because they were inside my purse and I wasn't about to stop, fish them out, and find my water bottle to flush them down.

"Just keep going," I said out loud, giving the words extra gravity.

There appeared to be no streetlights because the area around me grew dark and darker, a mix of gray and black shadows. In the distance, a smudge of fluorescent orange against the jagged black sky looked like part of a sign that might advertise the hotel that might have a restaurant. Moisture seeped through my thin jacket and the sweatshirt underneath as I continued toward the neon smear. It was a beacon, guiding me to a set of hotel doors. By then, my hair was hanging in damp strings around my face and my skin was wet from moisture.

How many times had I seen my often-homeless daughter look the exact same way: bedraggled and lugging around all her worldly possessions behind her? It was a gritty desperate feeling even though unlike her or the clients at the soup kitchen where I took students, there were three credit cards in my wallet that could buy me a hotel room for the night.

I cracked open one of the doors and strains of soft music and the light aroma of good food drifted through the air, but when I approached the hostess perched just inside, she said there were no tables available.

"You could sit at the bar—they serve food," she offered.

Eating alone wasn't normally a big problem for me—I had to do it often when I traveled for work, but this wasn't a "normal" time. The receptionist's finger, which ended in a slightly curved, highly polished fingernail, pointed toward a bevy of well-dressed twenty-somethings clustered around a waist-high circle of gleaming wood, holding fancy drinks.

Anxiety pulsed like a flashing sign around my neck as I took a step forward, dragging my suitcase. Did I imagine everyone was staring at me, an older woman wearing casual clothes and burdened with baggage? Hunger made me decide I didn't care, and after stashing my bags under the only empty high barstool, I discovered a decent menu and the kind of cold beer that comes with flecks of ice floating in it.

In other circumstances (i.e. Paul being alive), I would have lingered, sipping my drink and ordering dessert while I chatted with him on my phone. Instead, I slumped down in my seat and pretended to check emails. Grime that was a mix of sweat and fog coated my face and clung to my clothes, creating an even sharper contrast between me and what looked like a posh crowd of young professionals gathered for an after-work drink.

Of course, they weren't really looking at me or commenting on my bedraggled appearance, but I imagined each rolled eye and murmur was just that. I gulped down two beers and my salad and tipped the bartender generously before heading out to see if I could find my way back to the train station. I had very low confidence in my ability to go the right way, since as those close to me know, I am seriously challenged in the wayfinding area. Another thing I didn't have to worry about on the train.

After a wrong turn and several tense minutes, I found my way back to the station and navigated the maze of hallways that led to the waiting room. A combination of the alcohol and fatigue made me drift in and out of semi-sleep as I resumed my previous position, perched on the top of my suitcase. The Capitol Limited, my next train, would take me across Ohio and on to Chicago—but we didn't leave until early morning. Only the smallest of children had any energy left by the time we were finally invited to go out on the platform and board.

"Cheryl? Cheryl Dellasega?" a conductor called as I stumbled out of the brightly lit waiting room. Had something bad happened?

"That's me," I said, struggling toward him. He checked my name off on a clipboard, and then, to my delight, took the handle of my suitcase.

"I'm Charlie. I'll be your porter to Chicago," he said over his shoulder, climbing into a train car twice as tall as the ones I usually rode. He continued up a flight of stairs and turned right, leading the way to my "roomette," a tiny bed that was really just a double train seat flipped horizontally and covered with sheets and a blanket.

Charlie asked if I wanted my suitcase stored in the luggage rack and gave me a quick orientation to the train's layout. As soon as he left, I checked out all the switches and compartments and discovered that everything had an economic and efficient purpose. The curtains were lined with Velcro, so they sealed out any light, the handle on the door was also a lock, and the headboard was really part of the seat cushion.

It was delightful to pad to the tiny utilitarian bathroom a few roomettes away and shed the top layer of clothes I had worn since morning. There was a small toilet angled to make best use of the space, a single sink over a locked storage cabinet, and a stand-up shower shielded by a plain, thin plastic curtain. It would be interesting to take a hot shower in the morning with the floor rocking back and forth beneath me, but for the time being, I washed my face and brushed my teeth, which was enough to make me feel like I'd spent the day at a spa.

Back in my roomette, I plugged in my phone, wiggled out of the base layer of my clothes and into a clean t-shirt and sweatpants. Just as I slid under the covers, the sound of someone arriving in the hallway made me peer out of my half open door where I saw a middle-aged couple in the aisle, in the kind jolly mood usually associated with alcohol.

"Isn't this somethin'?" the woman asked, thrusting her camera phone at me. "Can you take a picture, darlin'?"

"Our kids won't believe this," the man said, tapping a ledge above the bed. "Which one of us has to sleep up here?"

"Oh sugar, let's snuggle in the bottom one," the woman said, and then giggled.

Although the ledge above their bed, like mine, was technically the place where a second person could sleep ("up top"), it was hard to imagine any adult actually doing that. The diagram in the Amtrak brochure couldn't do justice to the arrangement, which would require scaling a narrow little ladder to get up there—hopefully while the train was on steady stretch of track--then turning sideways and inserting your body into the bunk at the top.

"Please be quiet. We have other guests who are sleeping." Charlie the conductor reappeared, his brown eyes solemn.

He looked first at me, holding the camera, and then at them. I snapped the picture and slid my door shut again, and, after a few more muffled sounds, the newcomers settled in.

Despite the late hour and the pill that usually made me drowsy, I couldn't fall asleep. The car's cradle-like rock and the engine's steady vibration were soothing, and I had my favorite "white noise" app on my cellphone, but now that it was possible to sleep, I couldn't.

More than one person has described me as "fiercely independent," but underneath, I was not. Everything I had accomplished in the last two decades had been possible because of Paul. He had encouraged me to go back to school, and when there was work-related travel, he rearranged his schedule to watch the children if needed. He was almost always at home, waiting for me to call when I stayed at the office late or in a hotel far away.

"I wish you were here," I whispered, but unlike the shifting and creaking of my house, which seemed to signal his presence, the lullaby sounds of the train were unfamiliar. The black beast sped on into the pitch of night, soon to leave Pennsylvania, the state where Paul and I had lived for our entire married life.

I realized I was holding my cellphone as if poised to dial my husband and share those thoughts.

"You would not believe the guy I met on the train," I would add, had there been a Paul to call. "He was like a super spy, snooping on this guy behind me who talked nonstop from Harrisburg to Pittsburgh at the same time as he drilled me with all these questions."

"What kind of questions?" Paul would ask.

"Uncomfortable questions, like about you."

Imagining Paul at the other end of the phone made those last images of him pop open in my mind like a PowerPoint lecture. Although it happened far less frequently than in the early days after his death, once the first memory surfaced, the others inevitably followed.

Click. He was lying at the bottom of the steps, unresponsive.

Click. My son Joe's face was stunned as the ambulance crew struggled to get the loaded stretcher up the stairs.

Click. There was the Hospital Chaplain, my coworker, not knowing what to say when he came to the family waiting room just moments after Joe and I arrived.

"How can I help?" he had asked.

We were in shock and unsure of the next step. After looking at Joe to see if he had any ideas, I had suggested that the chaplain might be able to find out when we could see Paul, who was in the trauma room. It was a crumb of information that offered hope, since we hadn't received a prognosis.

Click. The ER resident physician held up the CT scan of Paul's brain, filled with blood. He said, "I'm going to give him an IV steroid that reduces brain swelling. It might make a difference, but I doubt it. There's hardly any chance he could return to baseline."

Click. My coworkers arrived at the Neurological Intensive Care Unit after the medicine had no effect and Paul was transferred out of the ER. I hugged everyone, even though I wasn't especially close to some of them.

Click. My daughter arrived from the prison to say goodbye to her father.

Click. Dead.

Gone forever.

alliance, ohio
the capitol limited

I was still awake when we crossed the border between Pennsylvania and Ohio. In the darkness of my roomette, full of as much sedation as was safe to take, my brain was speeding along with the train. I imagined the small towns of Ohio peeling away behind us: Sewickley, New Brighton, Beaver Falls, Columbiana, Canton, and Elkhart. Many were clones of Lewistown, teetering on an economy obliterated by Wal-Mart.

I knew those towns because I had driven through them many times. The summer after I completing my PhD, a senior faculty member at Penn State nominated me for a prestigious ten-week postdoctoral program, taking me completely by surprise since one had been interested in my professional advancement before. When I ended up being selected for the program and assigned to work on a project in Cleveland, it was great news for my career, but terrible for the family. By then, Paul had taken a new job back in Harrisburg and was commuting an hour every day from Lewistown while I went the opposite direction to State College every morning. To make matters worse, the lovely grandmotherly woman who watched our children throughout the school year had gone south for the summer, leaving us without childcare.

It was another one of those moments when I asked myself if the effort would really be worth the time and money. Although I worked part-time in the summers, I loved the academic calendar and being more available to my children for a few months of the year, but Paul refused to consider me turning down the opportunity. Instead, we sat down at the kitchen table after the children were in bed and cobbled together a plan.

"I'll come out there with the kids for a week," he said. "It'll be a vacation."

"In Cleveland?" I countered.

"They won't know the difference. Can you negotiate to work four ten-hour days and be back here on Fridays?"

The idea was taking hold in my mind. "Probably, and there's a nursing student who told me she would be in the area for the summer...she has a car, too."

The stipend from the program wouldn't cover all the plane tickets I needed to go back and forth, along with the cost of additional daycare. There was a train available, but the timing didn't work out, so we decided I would drive the 500 mile trip half of the time and fly the rest. Fortunately, there was a nice residential hotel not far from where I would be working.

In the end, that experience ended up being a huge success. I was the star of the program, producing more research than anyone else and pleasing the Penn State professor who had nominated me. Even better, my children loved their week in Cleveland, along with a local delicacy: pepperoni bread. They were also fond of the nursing student I hired to care for them and seemed to show no signs of missing me during the days when I was away.

Throughout our time together, Paul had been my biggest cheerleader in many ways. Although my parents chided me for not "staying at home and taking care of my children," he understood why I had the urge to get a PhD and carve out an academic career. When I was the first person in my department to be tenured in a decade, he threw a big party to celebrate, and on the nights when I had to stay at work late to finish an article or a grant or a presentation, he was there to watch the children.

"When I'm overwhelmed, I just plough through and do the work," he told me more than once, which proved to be wise advice.

There was another unique thing about Paul. He was the only person who could truly understand the heartbreak of our daughter, who had struggled for years with an eating disorder and addictions, which I wrote about, along with the anguish other mothers experienced, in my first book, *Surviving Ophelia*. There were many nights when we just held each other in bed, and although I would be the one crying, he may have been the one who hurt more because he held his feelings in.

Within a week of Paul's death, I had to go to court without him for my daughter's jail sentencing. When the judge gave her a lenient sentence, I said a prayer of thanks from my hard bench in the courtroom, remembering the moment when I looked at my husband in the Neurological Intensive Care bed and asked myself, "Who else will ever take care of her like we did?"

That judge had given her a chance, but throughout the year after Paul's death, she had fared worse than me, if such a thing was even possible. She had lived in a sometimes life-threatening crisis, including the catastrophe that took me to one of the worst neighborhoods in Harrisburg with a police escort. Fortunately, they rescued her from the former boxer who was holding her hostage and beating her up every day. The details of her kidnapping put me in a state of shock because I expected no pain to be worse than the loss of Paul, but that was just the beginning of many solo parenting challenges I would face.

Lying on my back, staring up at the dark ceiling above me on the train, I imagined Paul's face: the lines at the corner of his eyes pulling downward, the furrows of worry on his forehead, and the way he walked with his shoulders stooped, even when he wasn't carrying anything. In the year before his death, there seemed to be an aura of gloom around him, like a castle moat that no one could scale. Had he sensed something was going to happen?

Death had always been a topic that interested us, but in a hypothetical way. For some reason, we talked about it more in the months before he died, often debating what heaven would be like and what the other person would do when left alone. He wasn't a practicing Catholic, but told me that should the situation arise, he wanted last rites, "just in case." (He got them.)

"You'll get remarried right away if I go first," he said, more than once.

"No, you will. You're a good catch," was my standard response.

"Nope. I'll build a statue of you in the backyard, and every night after work, I'll go out and look at it and pine." Typical Paul humor.

"Well, be sure to cover it up when you bring my replacement around," I would counter.

The conversations seemed funny at the time.

Maybe our heightened awareness of life's end came from the work I was still doing. Not long after I stopped teaching Death

& Dying, I transferred to a different job and began to work with two other researchers interested in end-of-life care. For months, I ran focus groups to explore how people prefer to die, and when I was assigned as a small group facilitator in an ethics course for medical students, the continuum of death topics discussed was not so different from that long ago course I taught undergraduates: discussing the ethical aspects of euthanasia, how much effort to prolong life is too much (or not enough), and how do physicians handle their own struggles with loss and grief? Without intending to, my job had made me well acquainted with death.

Or had grief become a reality for Paul and me in the months before he died because of our connection to Patricia and Rick, a slightly older couple we met when we moved to Hershey? From the start, the two of them were mentors, friends, and spiritual companions. Patricia was a Midwestern farmwoman who worked hard at whatever job landed in front of her and never complained. Rick had been a teacher who worked his way up and into the Pennsylvania Department of Education.

Early on, Patricia had been diagnosed with cancer of the mouth, which made me worry even though she assured me her physicians weren't concerned about the new lumps that kept appearing on her palate. She didn't push for treatment because she was more concerned about Rick, whose health was declining from Parkinson's disease.

As I had seen happen many times before in my clinical work, her health got put on the back burner while she tended to the more immediate needs of caregiving for a beloved spouse who was steadily losing his ability to eat and walk. For years, Patricia did the job of three nurses, cooking special foods and taking her husband for physical therapy to preserve the function he had left. Paul and I joined in the caregiving efforts, visiting often and helping out where we could.

One night as we walked to our car after trying to help feed Rick, Paul shook his head.

"If that happens to me, pull the plug," he said. "I couldn't live like that."

"There isn't always a plug to pull. Look at Rick. There's nothing more that can be done to make him better, but there's also nothing to end his suffering."

"I don't care, just get me pain meds and pull the plug."

When Rick died, it was bittersweet to know that he was relieved of the physical symptoms he coped with so heroically. Patricia assured me that she was ready to focus on her own health, but by then she was fragile and strained.

Before long, she was the one sleeping in the hospital bed with hospice nurses visiting to give her pain medications and address any concerns the family had. I went to Patricia's house frequently and will never forget a time when I volunteered to do night duty so her daughter might get some sleep.

In the early hours of the morning, Patricia made a small sound.

"What can I do?" I went to her side instantly.

"It hurts so bad," she said. "Could you lay down next to me for a few minutes?"

"Of course." I squeezed into the bed and moved as close as possible given the narrow mattress and equipment attached to her. It was not quite time for her next pain med and even if it had been, Patricia accepted only the most minimal of doses.

"Your hands are so cool." She put my hand over the left side of her abdomen and sighed. "That feels good."

We stayed that way until she fell back asleep, but after a short time, she woke again.

"Do you see that angel that you got Rick?" she asked. "I put it on the dresser so it would be in front of me all the time."

I am known for my collection of angels, and sure enough, I recognized the small figurine positioned close to the footboard of her bed.

Patricia went on. "What do you think it will be like at the end?"

Although we had met at church, we had never discussed our religious views, but I didn't hesitate to respond. "I believe it will be wonderful. Rick will be there, and lots of angels."

She gave a tiny sigh and drifted off to sleep again. Somehow, I knew she was near to the end of her life.

The next morning, I went home to babysit my granddaughter, who wanted to help make her favorite chocolate chip cookies. After sliding the first batch in to bake, we watched cartoons until the timer rang.

"Cookies done," my granddaughter said, sliding off the sofa.

"They're too hot right now. You can watch TV for a few more minutes."

I went to the kitchen and opened the oven door to take them out, instantly blasted by a burst of heat that surged through my body with a roar like a strong gust of wind. It wasn't the familiar feeling of hot air escaping from an oven set to 350 degrees; I was so shaken I had trouble removing the cookie sheet.

As I leaned on the counter trying to compose myself, the phone rang.

"She's gone," Patricia's daughter said.

Could the strange searing sensation have been Patricia, saying goodbye? My sister, Beth, would have no trouble believing that it was, but I was the scientist. If someone described that kind of experience to me, my factual brain would attribute it to fatigue and emotion, not knowing that in the months after Paul died, I would come to question that philosophy.

The exact day when Mark, my friend and a virtual recluse, showed up to visit after Paul died is not as important as the fact that he did come to my house and what he told me. It was a shock to find him at my front door, transformed from an eccentric artist with wild hair, a grizzled beard, and paint-splattered clothes into a soft-spoken middle-aged man, neatly groomed and carrying a bottle of good white wine in one hand and a triptych of a cross he created in the other.

"How are you?"

He said it more as an acknowledgement of what had happened than an inquiry, going directly to the kitchen and somehow knowing where to find a corkscrew and two glasses. I drifted after him, accepting the drink he offered without hesitation, even though it was the middle of the afternoon.

Over a period of several years, Paul and I had bought some of Mark's art, which featured angels and other religious figures. I visited his house, which did double duty as a studio, from time to time, intrigued by the stacks of completed canvases inside every room. In addition to his mystical paintings, he had memorabilia from all over the world, collected during his early career in the military.

Although he barricaded himself from his neighbors, Mark, like my sister, Beth, was comfortable with the spirit world and the supernatural, which permeated his creativity. He told me about the dark magic of Brazil and a haunted house in Lancaster where he had lived briefly.

"I was pissed, man, those people rented their house to me, and it was full of ghosts, the kind you don't want to tangle with," he said. "They knew it, too."

Mark and I drank most of the bottle of wine that afternoon while curled up in my family room, not far from the wall where the first picture we had bought from him was hanging. Since I was barely choking down enough calories to keep going, the alcohol hit me quickly, a pleasant buffer against reality.

"You'll be fine," Mark said. "Don't worry about Paul. I saw him. He's happy."

My spine stiffened. "What?"

"Oh yeah, right after he passed, he came to me and told me he was really happy. Something about a boat, you and him rowing in a boat somewhere. Said it was really nice."

It didn't take long to locate the memory: after a particularly bitter period in our marriage where I turned to another man and it seemed we would divorce, both of us experienced an inexplicable change of heart. We decided to try again, and for a year, our relationship was like the dating days: exciting, fulfilling, and affectionate. In my heart, I believe he stopped drinking during those months.

At one point, we had gone to a local lake with our son and his girlfriend for a picnic and while there, rented a canoe. It was a really small boat on a really small lake, so circling it a few times was no great accomplishment, but the day was balmy and sunny, we were surrounded by happy people, and the future looked promising, for a change.

"But why did he come to you and not me? And why did he die? He shouldn't have." My voice had broken, but Mark waved me away.

"Forget that. You need to move on. You're going to live to be 86 and you've got lots of things to do."

Dismissiveness was a common behavior for Mark, since in the spirit world, there was no need for explanations, and nothing was beyond the realm of possibility. Although he never met my sister, they were alike in their beliefs about the unseen world. Then, not long after Mark visited, a pastor whose whole family had been especially supportive during the long years of my daughter's struggles contacted me.

Dr. Miller was a very grounded person and a physician. "The Prophetess is coming here to visit with us if you would like to talk to her," he said. It was a good thing we were on the phone, and he couldn't see my face, which was tight with astonishment.

"I don't know. I don't think I'm ready..." Ready for what?

Dr. Miller seemed to know.

"She'll be here on Sunday," Dr. Miller said. "I'll be glad to arrange it."

This man, his wife, and several of his adult children had been so reliable and spot on during many times of trouble that I trusted him implicitly. There was no part of me that felt a need to see "the Prophetess," but if he suggested it, I would do it.

"Okay," I said, and went to his house on Sunday afternoon where he ushered me into his study.

I read from the Bible just about every morning and right before turning in for the night. It was such a longstanding tradition that by then, I had probably gone through Genesis to Revelations at least twenty-five times, using different translations and approaches. At the mention of a "Prophetess," Deborah came to mind, a strong and wise woman in the Old Testament who led her tribe into battle. She was a judge who heard cases under a tree, and I've always imagined her as a big woman, bold and dramatic.

Evelyn was completely different. She seemed to float into Dr. Miller's study, so gaunt it was easy to see the outline of her shoulders under her clothes and the tendons in her neck. She wore a long flowing garment and wiry straw-colored hair flowed over her shoulders. Her eyes were like blue fire, focused and penetrating, but not unkind.

We sat next to each other, silent for a moment. I wasn't sure what she had been told but plunged ahead with what was most distressing at that moment.

"It's like my husband has been ripped out of my life," I said. "And nothing got to be resolved. It seems like he was drinking that morning, but I can't believe that. A .3 BAC at 6:30 in the morning?"

"What else?"

"The IRS is calling constantly and mailing me letters threatening to garnish my wages. Apparently Paul wasn't current on our taxes. My entire family is in the middle of some kind of crisis."

"Can you try talking to Paul?" Evelyn asked gently.

"I'm so upset with him, I can't even do that." My eyes, rarely dry in those days, filled with tears. I had gotten past the sobbing stage when Paul's name was mentioned, but that didn't mean I wasn't constantly emotional.

"Then talk to Jesus instead," she said, "Can you do that?"

"I guess."

I felt incredibly disappointed that Evelyn hadn't offered me a magical solution for seeing a way to move forward. Didn't I talk to Jesus every time I said a prayer? When she laid her hand on my shoulder, signaling an end to our discussion, I thanked her, even though I wasn't at all grateful.

"Think about what I said," she told me as I headed out the door toward my car.

Paul's cremains were in a beautiful wooden box that I had placed on the table next to the bed as soon as I received it. Surrounding it with artifacts became an obsession. I added cards people had sent, figurines, rosary beads, a handwritten Kiddush, a square of gauze with his blood on it that the ambulance crew left behind, and plenty of candles. At night, it was comforting to slip away from reality with Lacey at my feet, watching the shadow of the flickering flames dance across the bedroom wall.

The night after I saw the Prophetess, her words came to mind when I lit the candles, as if she was encouraging me again to imagine that Jesus was right there and I could talk to Him. That felt ridiculous, so I focused on the altar I had made. Leaning against the box was a prayer card with a picture of Jesus on it. He looked like a kindly white man with a lamb tucked under one arm and a staff held upright in the other—probably not an accurate depiction, but I decided to go with it.

"How can I cope with supporting myself and our children without Paul's help? And I mean that in a lot of ways—emotional and financial."

It was strange to hear the words I'd been thinking spoken aloud, as if someone was really listening. With the same disappointment I felt after meeting Evelyn, I gave up after advice one try. The candles were real, a "prophetess" was not. Even the Bible didn't have many of them.

I fell asleep (or at least it seemed that way) and suddenly Paul was there, looking much as he had when we met on our first date. He had more hair and was wearing faded jeans and an untucked worn, checkered red flannel shirt that he loved. The expression on his face was relaxed, much as it had been on the night when we were introduced by our best friends.

In the dream, if that's what it was, I was sitting below him, in some kind of boat, surrounded by other people. He was on the pier, watching me.

"How could you do this, Paul?" I said. "I need your help, and you know it!"

"But I am there, Cheryl," he said with a half-smile. "I'm with you all the time."

"No you're not! You're really not!"

"Oh yes I am." He leaned over and playfully tickled my ribs as he used to do on very rare times when he publicly displayed affection. "You just can't see me, but I'm there."

The mannerisms and the way he delivered the response were so like him that I startled awake with an angry retort ready. Lacey had shifted into standing position, her black button eyes alert, but she hadn't growled or seemed worried, which is what Westies do best. I reached down and rubbed the spot between her ears, as much for her comfort as mine, and we both settled back into sleep position.

Paul had been there. The dream/vision/visitation was so real I could feel where he touched me, and even when I woke, the conversation was still going on.

From that point on, our house seemed alive with his presence. I would hear his heavy tread on the stairs in the morning at the time when he usually got ready for work. Just as I began to get out of bed and remind him that he needed to be home by a certain time, the realization would hit: no one was on those stairs. Other strange things happened in the house where we had lived for over a decade. Our bedroom was connected to the family room, an unusual arrangement which meant any conversations were likely to be overheard through the door. At nighttime, I would hear Paul's voice, a distinctive low rumble that sounded like a cordial talk with Joe. The first time this happened, I got up and opened the door to find the TV silent and the family room dark. Thereafter, I didn't bother to investigate.

A short time later, Paul appeared to me again, this time without my questions or prompting. It was nighttime, and I had fallen asleep, but suddenly, he was standing on the far side of the bed, dressed in the same attire as in the first dream about him. This time, he wasn't playful.

"Why are you here? What do you want?" My question came out as a mix of irritation and longing.

"I need your forgiveness," he said.

During his lifetime, Paul rarely admitted to wrongdoing or apologized, which was the basis of many complaints on my part. Asking for forgiveness was probably the most stunning thing he could say. I hesitated, but then, in the same way it would have happened in real time, my heart softened.

"Of course I forgive you."

He vanished then, with an almost audible whoosh, much like the one I felt pass through me after Patricia's death. It would be the last time I encountered him in that setting and at the time, felt like one more loss has piled on to an already precarious stack of misfortunes.

chicago
the empire builder

Finally, I slept that first night on the train like I used to when my dad drove on long family trips and my brother, sister, and I were stretched out in our allotted spaces in the back of our mega station wagon. The three of us would tussle and quarrel until we fell asleep, secure in the knowledge that our father was in charge and would get us to our destination safely; that's how I felt as we headed to Chicago.

When I awoke and checked the time, it was too late to make the last breakfast, but too early for lunch. My stomach rumbled in protest, but I was still tired and a bit hungover from the sleeping medication, which made it hard to climb out of the tiny bed. As I lay there trying to get motivated, there was the sound of small feet running back and forth in the corridor that ran the length of the car. This continued for about five minutes, accompanied by childish shrieks of laughter and shouts.

"This is your porter speaking. Please monitor your children. All parents are expected to attend to their children at all times." I recognized Charlie's voice over the public address system, firm and fatherly, but to no avail. The pound of footsteps up and down the stairs continued. He tried a second time as I was gathering up my shower things.

"Ladies and gentlemen, there is to be no running in the aisles or corridors and no children without adult supervision. Parents will be asked to leave the train if they cannot control their children."

That seemed to work. The footsteps stopped, or at least for as long as it took me to locate my suitcase and pull it out for another change of clothes.

As I zipped it shut, the cover split completely.

"Damn." I swear so rarely that there's a strange satisfaction to it when I do. Fortunately, the Chicago layover would be long enough for a quick shopping trip, so I reallocated my belongings to my purse, my backpack, and a plastic laundry bag I discovered in the bathroom. I took a gloriously long and hot shower hoping no one was waiting outside in the hallway and thankful we were on a fairly steady track.

Some of my fatigue washed away with the shower water and now that we were on our way, it felt exciting. Maybe I could even jumpstart a new life that wouldn't involve a daughter who was back in jail—she would be miraculously better. It wouldn't involve so many fender benders that my automobile insurer would threaten to cancel my policy—I would be a safe and focused driver. I wouldn't give my children large sums of money that I thought they needed—I would have a balanced budget that allowed me and them to live comfortably.

Rash behaviors and bad judgment, not unusual among those dealing with major life challenges, would be a thing of the past because on the train. I was going to hit that mythical "reset" button I knew existed. Weren't there countless books and research papers assuring me that it was always possible to change your life?

For the first time in months, I felt optimistic and removed from the day when I told Kathy, my widow mentor, that it seemed impossible to go on.

"I'll never be happy again," I said.

That was a kind of despair I had never experienced, but by then, my daughter had been in and out and back in jail, my finances were a mess, and my relationship with Lacey and my granddaughter seemed like the only healthy things in my life. On the train, there was a growing distance between me and the mess my world had become since Paul died. I was even enjoying a bit of luxury, since being a "sleeper" passenger was like flying first class, something I've experienced only twice. As a premium, there was Charlie, who dedicated himself to the roomette section, functioning as a combination of host and housekeeper. He did his job well; there was a pretty constant supply of coffee and ice water on a table bolted into the wall of the second floor.

During one of the early morning stops, my neighbors had changed. The compartment next to me—the same size as—mine—now contained a family of five, first glimpsed when I was on the way back from my shower. The three young girls were extremely well behaved—definitely not the hall runners. They were curled up on the bottom berth with their mother.

When we exchanged pleasantries and began to chat, I complimented her on how quiet her children were. She tipped her head in the direction of the top bunk.

"My husband is a pastor. He's going to be ordained in his first church. We just have a few more stops."

I wasn't sure whether that related to my compliment or was a segue into conversation. We talked a bit about the life of a "church wife," and then I remembered that I hadn't eaten.

"Do you think I can get any breakfast upstairs?" I asked her. "I slept through breakfast."

My new friend gave a tiny sniff. "I think they stick to their routine. It seemed like they were pretty anxious to get us in and out."

"Then hopefully the café car will open soon. I really have to get something to eat. Nice talking to you." I smiled at the little girls and gave them a wave of my hand. "Have fun on the rest of your trip!"

Grabbing my laptop and purse, I headed for the dining car, passing through cars of two-storied sleepers. Roomettes were the smallest option; other compartments had their own bathroom and shower. There were even some rooms that were the equivalent of a miniature dorm room—the most luxurious arrangement.

As I passed by one of the suites with an open door, it looked like a family gathering was taking place inside. The sounds from within made me pause for a second with a throb of loneliness, hearing that mix of laughter, joking voices, and queries from young children that had once been a part of my life.

"Mommy? Are we there yet?"

"Why can't I go run in the hall again?"

"I'm hungry. Is it almost lunch time?"

I came to the dining car, which was like an old-fashioned diner on wheels, complete with hard plastic tables, bench style seating, and windows the size of a large screen TV. A group of employees were sitting at one table with cups of coffee in front of them.

"Is there any way I could get some food?" I asked the woman seated nearest to the aisle.

She looked up and I knew instantly that I had made a mistake. Her tablemates give me the once over and lifted their eyebrows slightly.

"I'm on break. You'll have to wait for lunch or go to the café when it opens," the woman said.

After a painful silence, I apologized for interrupting and moved on, suspecting they must sigh often about stupid passengers who don't know the rules of long-distance travel. Or maybe it was my appearance: still wet hair (air-drying it was a longstanding habit), a short-sleeved t-shirt and cut off sweatpants, with flip-flops that revealed my manicured toenails. Hardly the well put together traveler.

The café was closed but the menu boasted an impressive assortment of convenience foods as well as beer. I moved on to the Observation Car to wait until it opened.

It was a marvel—the train version of a glass diving bell. You could sit in a comfortable chair or at a table and do nothing more than look out the windows on all sides or lean back and see landscape and sky rolling by like a video on fast forward. If that wasn't entertaining enough, there were plenty of interesting people to watch—the same group of Amish travelers from the Pittsburgh train station were there, along with their cooler. A tour guide lectured an assortment of people who were gathered around her like a church congregation, and there were also a few solos with no apparent companion—like me.

That was another time when I would have called Paul. We would talk about my trip and perhaps reminisce about the many times we visited his parents in Evanston, just a bit outside of Chicago. Instead, I sat with my laptop unopened, still disoriented but content to look at scenery until we reached our next stop.

We got there before the café opened, but I discovered that as a "sleeper" passenger, I was entitled to use a lounge at Union Station, which made the waiting room at Pittsburgh look like a slum. It was new, clean, and stocked with fresh fruit and bottled water. I grabbed an apple and bit into it gratefully.

Like everyone else, I have special places that make me feel connected to loved ones. Whether it's the local restaurant frequented on the occasional nights out, a childhood home, or the site of an annual family reunion, these locales take on new significance when a loved one who was part of those memories dies. Instead of a happy reflection on times spent there, the place becomes a bittersweet reminder of what will be no more.

Chicago, where Paul's parents lived during the early years of our marriage, had been like a New York City getaway during our State College/Lewistown years when we needed to escape rural Pennsylvania. Paul's dad, Joe Senior, loved being a grandfather and father-in-law and always welcomed us with love and plans for special excursions that would make our visits memorable. Marie, Paul's mom, was the complete opposite. She wasn't affectionate or especially kind but did end up becoming an unexpected widow role model for me.

Shortly after she and Joe Senior moved to the Hershey area, she courageously battled breast cancer while caring for him. When he died, she forbade anyone to cry at the funeral mass, which she reluctantly held at the local Catholic church. (She despised organized religion, although it was never completely clear why.)

She forged her way through so many difficulties I thought maybe she would have some advice for me. One time I asked her, "With everything that's going on, do you believe there's a God?"

She stopped what she was doing and eyed me coldly. "Of course not. Look at all the starving children in the world."

There was no crying from her when Paul died, either. I later learned from my children that she blamed me for his death because I traveled too much and left him alone, which wasn't surprising since she often urged me to follow the model of Navy marriage she and Joe Senior had. A wife was supposed to entertain and make social connections that helped her husband, not pursue her own career. Still, I couldn't deny that she was far more stoical during hardships than me. Did her atheism make her more pragmatic and resilient, with no expectations beyond the challenges of everyday life?

When I went to sit down in the train station lounge, my purse slid down on my arm and the zipper gave way—most likely because it was too full, just like my self-destructed suitcase the night before. Luckily, I was able to check my belongings at the station for a small fee and begin what the ticket agent assured me was "a short walk" to downtown.

After two blocks, I was full of memories from the era when our children were young and Paul and I would make the westward trek with them, always going downtown to admire the Sears tower, visit the aquarium, check out the museums, and walk along the Riverwalk, weather permitting. I'm not sure why we crammed so many activities into the short time we were there, since our kids were inevitably cranky and uncooperative by the end of the day. Now they remember those times fondly, but in the moment, it seemed crazy to take them anywhere that required packing up the stroller and diaper bag.

Is there any way I can escape Paul? I thought as I stretched my legs out in long strides over the wide sidewalk. After twenty minutes of brisk walking without coming any closer to familiar scenery, I flagged a taxi and asked to be driven to a place where I could shop.

"You mean like a shopping center?" The cabbie twisted in his seat to give me a skeptical look.

"No, downtown. Just a store," I said, but there were no places that I recalled as "just a store" where an ordinary shopper like me might go. In fact, I had a vague memory of trying to buy diapers in downtown Chicago one time and striking out completely.

The cabbie dropped me off on a block where several pricey boutiques were tucked in between office buildings, but after browsing through them, the price tag for my trip flashed in my memory. Perhaps a second backpack or sports bag would be an economical option.

Then, the bright pink of a Hello Kitty store caught my eye. Prominently displayed in the window were several suitcases my granddaughter would love. Since she would be doing some traveling later in the summer, having a suitcase for use on my trip which I could pass on to her was the perfect choice. When I noticed a scratch on the leather of the smallest bag, the clerk knocked off 10%. My final tab was $120.00—more than I wanted to spend, but time was running out and I had no options.

Back in the lounge of the Chicago train station, I transferred all my belongings out of the plastic bag and into the new pink and brown suitcase emblazoned with a smiling white kitten, pleased with the result. Then I settled in to wait for my train, trying to ignore the sideways glances of other passengers in the lounge. They were stereotypical "mature" couples with salt and pepper hair, slightly overweight, and dressed in leisure clothes. The woman immediately next to me asked where I was headed, and it turned out she was going westward too, on a long planned post-retirement trip.

"We've been married thirty years," she said, patting her husband's arm. "You really get used to a person after all that time."

A quick calculation made me realize that Paul and I were together nearly as long as my new friends. That led to another insight: I wasn't much younger than the couples around me—in fact, if Paul was there, we would fit right in. We would be a stereotypical mature couple.

"We went on the train for an anniversary trip," she said. "And we loved it. Who would think you could have so much fun riding in a passenger car all day? Right, George?"

She gave her husband a small nudge with her elbow. He continued to read his newspaper, but smiled, perhaps to let her know he was listening.

In another setting, I might have played Lee and quizzed her about her life. Had they gone through bad years? What was the "glue" that kept them together for three decades? Did they have children? Maybe I would even share my "adventure within an adventure" theory of train travel.

Instead, she went to fix a cup of coffee and I noticed a brochure about The Empire Builder, my next train, on the end table next to me. Usually, train history was not my first interest, but as I paged through the booklet, I realized what a major accomplishment the hub of trains across the United States was.

A map similar to the one on the inside cover of my Amtrak System Timetable was reproduced in the booklet, crisscrossed with a net of red lines that represented all the possible train routes with all the possible numbers attached to them. You could get just about anywhere in the country by rail.

The Empire Builder, built in 1928 to connect Chicago with the west, was responsible for the growth of our country, allowing goods to flow more quickly from one coast to the other. Constructed with sheer physical manpower, the trails covered thousands of miles of tracks that were first used by horse drawn carts and then steam engines.

Chicagoan James Hill, a tycoon who pushed forward the laying of rails, reminded me of Milton Hershey, the founder of the chocolate company my hometown was named for. Both men built homes for their workers and seemed to genuinely care about the people who helped them succeed. By the time I finished browsing the booklet and skimmed the free newspapers scattered around the lounge, it was time to board.

It felt like saying goodbye to another little piece of the past as we pulled out of Chicago's Union Station. Yes, I would come through on the return trip, but not long enough to go back downtown and remember how often I had been there with Paul. That was probably just as well. With each stop further west there was more distance from my roots on the east coast and the life I built with Paul. From this point on, it would be new territory with no ties to the past—or so I thought.

wisconsin, minnesota, north dakota
the empire builder

I got my first real train meal that evening as we crossed through the lush land of lakes that was northern Wisconsin. Other than some fruit in the lounge and a quick sandwich in Chicago, I hadn't eaten anything substantive, and to my surprise, I felt ravenously hungry. When our server brought out rolls and foil wrapped rectangles of real butter, it was all I could do not to grab two of each and devour them in a few bites. We ate family style, though, and I was seated across from a woman and two young girls I presumed to be her daughters.

I gulped down one roll slathered with butter and drank half a glass of water to fill up my stomach while the younger girl, sitting across from me, shredded her bread onto her plate. Meanwhile, her sister broke hers in pieces and ate it. It was hard not to eye the one left in the basket, which I assumed the mother wasn't going to eat because her attention was focused on the glass of water she sipped in the same way other women might drink an expensive glass of wine.

"I'm Veronica," the woman said, "and these are my girls, Lily and Vanessa. Girls, say 'hi' to the nice lady." They did. "We're headed back home in Minnesota. Where are you going?"

"Cross country," I said. "I'm Cheryl."

Veronica looked beyond me, her eyes glistening. She was a soft woman with a round body, smooth white skin and chestnut hair. Her voice had the trace of a Southern drawl.

"I just relocated my daddy to a nursing home because his health is failing. We had to go down and help settle up the house. I can't believe how bad he looked," she said.

She repeated the last line two more times as she picked up the last roll and played with it, rolling it between her fingers. Each time she said, "I can't believe how bad he looked," her daughters gave each other a quick look.

During a short stint as a visiting nurse, I experienced more about life and death than I would from all my time in the hospital as a critical care nurse. Two of my favorite female patients died slowly over the course of the year when I worked that job, along with other heartbreaks. Veronica was reminding me of a time when I arrived at the house of a delicate older woman named Sarah, one of my other favorite patients (I had many) and found her standing in the middle of what had been her dining room, every piece of china, silverware, and crystal glass she accumulated over her seventy years laid out on the floor.

"This is everything I own," Sarah said to me, her voice faltering. She was doing what Veronica referred to as "settling up" the house so she could join her elderly husband in a nearby nursing home. In a matter of days, she would move from an ancient Victorian home crammed with antiques to a two-room apartment in a nearby extended care complex. At the time of my visit, Sarah was preparing for her entire life to be auctioned off to the highest bidders.

How often had I visited my own great grandmother and marveled at her treasures: the pink glass dessert plates and crocheted doilies that she kept tucked away with her "good dishes" in a polished hutch? I had moved forward to touch Sarah's arm, but her middle aged daughter shook her head at me.

"This is for the best, Mom," she said, elbowing Sarah out of the room. No doubt, the funds raised along with the sale of the house would be used to pay Sarah's bills for a place where she didn't want to live. It was a hard decision, but my elderly patient was fragile and could no longer keep up the two-story home where she and her husband had raised six children.

The train waitress appeared with my entrée, a vegetarian selection that was literally cooked vegetables. I added some of the left-over butter and dug in.

"My mom died not too long ago, so now I guess he will too." Veronica had eyes so pale blue they were almost transparent; she was still lost in her thoughts, massaging bits of bread with her long fingers as Vanessa continued to play with her food.

"That's really a hard decision to make," I said.

"Have you ever lost anyone you loved?" Veronica shifted her gaze back to me and her daughters looked too, expectant.

"My husband died about a year ago."

"Why bless your heart." Veronica's eyes held mine for another second, and she repeated herself, "Bless your poor heart," then picked up a knife and cut Vanessa's steak.

Vanessa took her fork and pushed the pieces around on the plate. Lily, who had ordered fish, finished her food and dabbed at her lips, her eyes tracking momentarily toward her phone.

"If she doesn't eat that, I will," she said.

Veronica looked at her, and for a second it occurred to me that Lily looked nothing like her mother, while Vanessa did. Perhaps they weren't blood relations after all.

"Please eat, darling," Veronica said to Vanessa. "You need your meat."

Seeing her tend to the girl reminded me of my ministrations to my own daughter, who had once been like them, close to adolescence yet still with the innocent look of young children: clean faced, shiny haired, and slim bodied. Vanessa wore a purple shirt with a pink kitten on the front, and Lily kept her fingers, tipped with pale pink nail polish inches away from her sequined cellphone.

Very few people could understand the complex story of my daughter, and how her untroubled childhood had erupted when she was about Lily's age. Paul and I battled to help her with the best treatment centers in the country, but her life dissolved into a cycle of drugs, prison, and other unbelievable crises.

"She just has to hit bottom," we were told again and again. "Then she'll get better."

"What is 'bottom'?" Paul finally asked. "Isn't it being in jail for her birthday? Getting beat up by a thug? Nearly dying because she refuses to eat?"

We had mourned the course her life had taken nearly every day and been sure we would lose her for good more than a dozen times after being summoned to the ER in the middle of the night, but it seemed even her father's death and the awful five days she had spent mourning him by herself in jail would be that mythical "bottom." If anything, her life fell further apart in the year after he was gone.

Beyond the window, velvety green and brown land was dotted with lakes that looked like discs of silver tossed out at random.

The scenery sped by, a flat ribbon of landscape continuously unraveling, much as it had during a train trip Paul, the children, and I took across Sweden. There, too, the countryside had been unspoiled, dotted with natural and manmade beauty. Small villages bordered by trim trees and tidy roads were picture book perfect and the occasional billboard looked cleaner and brighter than the ones in the U.S.

Sweden had been a family honeymoon, made possible by an unusual opportunity extended through my position at the university, but one which I believed helped Paul and I reconnect with each other temporarily. It also allowed our children to glimpse a different culture and a way of life with a father who was less distracted and more attentive—his job was to take care of them while I did the work I had been sent to do. We were able to afford the month long stay because the organization that paid for me to be a visiting professor agreed to provide a free place for our family to live in the midst of a planned community.

Before traveling there, I had learned a bit about Sweden from some of the senior faculty, who shared many stories about deals brokered in a sauna, or new proposals confirmed with straight shots of aquavit and a naked plunge into a snowbank. I never thought there would be an offer for me to go there, but it turned out that the Swedes wanted a nurse who did geriatric research, and I was the only one available. While it seemed unlikely that Paul would want or be able to go to Sweden, especially for five weeks, he surprised me.

"I can go," he told me, after consulting with the partners at his law firm. "I can take three weeks off in August and then come back with the kids in time for them to start school and you can stay for an extra two weeks. Maybe your parents will come and help out."

That meant we could spend almost a month together in Sweden, so we got passports for the kids, bought two oversized suitcases, made arrangements for the dog to be taken care of, and took off on a memorable ten-hour plane trip. Being on a jet with three children who were grouchy and tired was the equivalent of a road trip that never ended, but it was soon behind us when we got to Stockholm and found playgrounds inside the airport.

When we arrived at our final destination, a university town in southern Sweden, my contacts picked the five of us up in two cars and transported us to the planned community where we would be staying. Briskly, they showed us around and took off, telling me the name of the bus I should take in the morning to get to the university. It was a bare minimum of a welcome.

We were all hungry since it was well past the time when our bodies expected dinner. I went over to the food store and quickly discovered our American dollars and Traveler's Checks weren't recognized and I had no Swedish money. I also had no phone numbers to call for help, but the goodness of a middle-aged woman who gave me a few krona tided us over for 24 hours until the banks opened.

Paul was a different person in Sweden—perhaps because it was almost impossible for him to get alcohol there (in an attempt to cut down on alcohol consumption, the liquor stores were open for a limited time each day, and the prices were even more shocking than the McDonald's coffee he refused to buy). It was a kid-friendly country too—we rode trains that had a playroom built into one car and provided access to even remote areas of the country, visited the community indoor water park frequently, had a day at the Tivoli amusement park, and did a lot of exploring.

Paul even took the children on a "cruise" to Finland and had a weekend by himself in Copenhagen, eager to explore and enjoy the rare opportunity to live abroad again. As a military brat, he had lived all over the world, a situation I thought was glamorous but which he hated because it meant starting over at new schools again and again. In Sweden, I found myself wondering what life might be like if he didn't have to work at a stressful job and we could make ends meet on my salary. Even the children seemed happier there—but perhaps that was because we all knew it was a temporary dream.

Not long after we were back from Sweden and the afterglow of a fairytale trip lingered, I asked Paul for any quarters he might have one morning. I needed them for the street meter because I was headed off to supervise nursing students at a nearby nursing home whose small parking lot I was forbidden to use. Half asleep, he plunged his hand into the pocket of his pants, which were hung next to the bed. When he pulled out a handful of change and extended it to me, there were pills mixed in with the money.

I was stunned. "What are those for?"

"Oh." He hesitated for a second, his eyes dazed. "They're left over from when I stopped drinking."

The Lewistown blackout that exposed his addiction had been years before, but I was in a hurry to get to work, so I couldn't quiz him just then. Later that evening when I brought the subject up, he shrugged his shoulders.

"Cheryl, what do you want from me?"

His tone of voice was the same as it had been during a weekend visit to my parents that we had made while dating.

"Cheryl, how much does Paul drink?" my father had asked, noting that the supply of beer in the refrigerator in the basement was dwindling rapidly.

Later, I confronted Paul. "My dad saw all the empty cans in the trash, and no one is drinking but you. He asked me what was going on."

"He checked the trash?" Paul rolled his eyes. "What's wrong with having a few beers?"

It was the same type of retort I would get in the future when I probed about empty bottles and cans. The combination of his tone and the way he gave a slight shake of his head made me feel like a nag and critic abou this alcohol intake. I stopped pushing, even though we both knew he was being dishonest.

Paul got regular bonuses and praise from his clients. He came home at the same time every night and ate dinner with his family. He paid the bills and went to church on Sundays. Given this evidence, at the time he posed the question, I wondered, *What more do I want from him?* One year after his death, I knew. I wanted the real Paul—the person I somehow knew was there behind the bottle, the man I had thought I glimpsed in Sweden.

east glacier park, montana
the empire builder

After a dinner on board followed by a few café beers, I went to my little bed where there was no television, radio, or cellphone reception. As dusk darkened into night, I could see the dim, slumbering dinosaur shapes of mountains, the twinkling streetlights of housing developments, and then, only the canopy of sky overhead, like a swath of black velvet backlit by tiny pricks of white.

If you wanted to star gaze, you could have slept outside in your own backyard and saved yourself a lot of money.

The mean voice hit on a truth. What had I gained from this trip where I was supposed to be getting away from Paul and start setting precedents for my new life? There was a list of to-dos that I had ignored: take pictures and videos to make a mini documentary when I returned, meet new people who could share their insights about life, read a few books, and do some writing that wouldn't be about Paul.

In addition to the absence of my tried-and-true coping strategy, I felt lonelier on a train full of people than in my Hershey bedroom. After Charlie, there was no friendly porter or fellow passenger to pierce the isolation, even when I hung out in the Observation Car hoping that would happen. Why were nights at home with Lacey more comforting than traveling someplace new and potentially exciting? According to my calculations, the trip out would be about 2805 miles and the return 2360. That should provide a lot of buffer between a person and her problems, but somehow, mine were still along for the ride, just like my toothpaste and hairbrush.

As the train car swayed westward on the tracks, I took out a paperback copy of *Agent Zigzag: A True Story of Nazi Espionage, Love, and Betrayal* by Ben Macintyre. The striking red and black designs imposed over the face of a man on the cover and the jacket description had intrigued me enough to pick it up in the bookstore for Paul some time ago, but I forgot to give it to him. Bringing it on the trip was a kind of tribute, since my late husband was a fan of World War II spy stories and often kept me intrigued with his knowledge of history. His law school buddies made me laugh with their memories of Paul reciting not only all the presidents but all the kings and queens of England.

The book was about Eddie Chapman, an incredibly talented real life double agent who fooled just about everyone he encountered. In one chapter, he was hobnobbing with the Germans, being trained to return to Britain and obtain secret information, and in the next, he was collaborating with the British to dupe the Germans when he returned to their headquarters in France.

As I turned the pages and wondered about Eddie Chapman's true personality, I couldn't help seeing parallels between him and Paul, despite their different circumstances. How could someone slip in and out of different personas so easily? Was it as simple as upbringing?

Paul's past, although not traumatic, had shaped the person he became. As a young boy, he had ear surgery which left him partially deaf, a condition that went undetected until years later—a possible reason for his introverted personality. Being a military brat and moving frequently hadn't added to his confidence.

"I would just get used to one place and we were on to another. Then my dad finally put down his foot so I could spend all of my high school years in one place," he told me soon after we met. I thought the years he spent in Italy and Ecuador and San Diego were exactly the kind of childhood I would have liked, but what he remembered was the terror of his first days as a new student, repeated again and again.

Then there was the alcohol. Until college, he hadn't broken any of the major "rules." He went to Mass every Sunday, worked during the summers, kept his curfew, and dated sporadically in high school. During the early weeks of his freshman year at college, though, he had gone to a party where they served hard liquor.

"I remember that first drink," he told me the night after his Lewistown blackout. It was the most honest conversation we would ever have about his addiction. "I took a swallow and felt it burn the whole way down to my stomach..." he said, lifting one hand to rest over the slight slope of his abdomen. "...and then this wonderful warmth just spread out over my body, and I was hooked."

"But what about the hangovers?" I had asked, thinking of my own early forays into drinking. "How could it ever be worth waking up the next day super sick?"

He shrugged, a careless movement I would see again and again signaled that he was finished talking about the topic, just as he would find explanations for every other aspect of his alcoholism. After consulting with a doctor to help him quit drinking, his hands continued to shake, but he attributed that to nerves. His slurred speech was due to "chewing ice," which supposedly suppressed his appetite even as he steadily gained weight. A myriad of small accidents occurred throughout our marriage: backing into my car one morning while pulling out of the driveway, rendering it undrivable; dropping his keys down an elevator shaft; and slamming the bathroom door at church into an elderly man who was exiting. Each incident would be accounted for with the same shrug and vacant look.

Lying in the train with my book resting across my chest, I thought about Eddie Chapman, who was a hero. How had people accepted his wildly improbable explanations for strange behavior? The entire British and Nazi militaries had been conned by him again and again. It was one matter to be a master of the sincere lie and the expert of earnest and honest deception when you were a soldier, but Paul, so functional and middle class, was also able to continue persuading me of the impossible. Apparently, the art of deception wasn't that hard if you looked "normal."

"There's not a day when I don't think about drinking," Paul had said during a time in Hershey when I thought he was abstaining.

The look on his face made me feel sorry for him, believing that he was in a constant battle to avoid alcohol, but after that lunch with his secretary Sue, I realized he hadn't said he wasn't drinking, just that he thought about it constantly. Those were the nuances that made me especially bitter in hindsight, adding to my grief shame. I couldn't feel sorry for him because I was still so angry, and only my therapist knew it. His family and coworkers certainly didn't need to have their memories of him tainted, nor did our children.

Mixed with my guilt about not being a genuine widow, i.e. the kind of spouse who could list all the wonderful things about her departed husband, was another kind of grief I hadn't expected. I came to believe I had failed Paul in the most important way possible. Instead of being a helpmate, I wore blinders, believing if there was a really serious problem he would confide in me, and we would solve it.

Of course he couldn't and I didn't—but if I had….I still questioned the accuracy of the BAC level drawn in the ER. It was hard to believe he was that drunk at 6:30 in the morning, although when I had greeted him in the kitchen, he had mentioned being awake since 2 a.m., not an unusual habit.

And don't forget, there was no alcohol on his breath when you did CPR, my internal voice added. No matter what facts surfaced, the logical, scientific part of my brain couldn't counter the suspicious, nagging Cheryl who knew the worst—Paul's speech had been slurred when we spoke on the phone the day before he died.

I had called him at work to check in about our plans for the evening, but after a few minutes of conversation, I switched the topic.

"Have you been drinking? You sort of sound like it." This was the way I broached any accusation—hoping to be discredited instead of criticizing. He didn't miss a beat with his response.

"Oh yes, I've been chewing ice. Even my clients have noticed it on the phone. My tongue gets numb." He even exaggerated "gets" into "geths" for emphasis.

What had he been thinking during those last seconds of his life, a man who carefully crafted a façade of function and normalcy? Did he lament, "Oh shit, now Cheryl will find out I really was drunk at work (again)?" Or had he lived his life in anticipation of getting caught? When did he learn how to dispose of alcohol bottles the minute they were empty and to drink his booze in a strong chaser like coffee?

Those questions brought back the sickening fragrance of Binaca, the breath spray which I encountered on the night we met when he casually pulled the little bottle out and squeezed a few drops onto his tongue every few hours. I thought he was worried about bad breath.

Why hadn't I brought something light and refreshing to read instead of a story that seemed a counterpoint to my life? I shut the book, tired of Eddie's character and tired of wondering about Paul but unable to use my phone to download anything else to read or watch.

During the day, there were regular stops where passengers could get out and pace the length of the platform for a few minutes, but the last one had been hours earlier. Needing to stretch my legs, I got up and wandered down the sleeper car's dimmed hallway. Somehow, I got disoriented and ended up in the "regular" car where the lights were also low, but passengers slept in the familiar upright seats I occupied on all the other times I took the train.

I paced the length of the dark car, marveling at the creativity used to craft sleeping arrangements. One little boy was stretched across two footrests, swaddled in blankets, with an arm dangled over the edge of his space while adults I assumed to be his parents slept sideways in the seats above him. Some people entwined themselves and reclined their seats to the max—were they lovers, family, or friends, with their bodies pressed so closely together to make the most of a tiny space? Other figures had earphones plugged into a device and a hood or blanket drawn over their heads.

When I returned to my car and popped a second sleeping pill, my brain still wouldn't shut down. As the train ploughed ahead through Minnesota and North Dakota like a boat on slightly choppy water, the swaying from side to side reminded me of happier days, when my children curled in my arms after nursing and fell asleep as I rocked them. My daughter in particular had loved to rest her head against my shoulder and pat my back.

Eventually, I drifted off, but for the rest of the night I continued to swim up from the dregs of sleep long enough to register where I was and then doze off again. Not surprisingly, I slept through breakfast (again) and ended up having a veggie burger and a Bud Light beer from the café when it opened mid-morning. Drinking alcohol that early in the day was something I had never done but being on a kind of vacation and all the sad circumstances that prompted it made the microwaved food and semi-cold beer satisfy my hunger and thirst perfectly.

For the rest of that morning, I sat in the Observation Car with my laptop turned on and watched my fellow passengers. The group of Amish travelers and their cooler were still on the train. Some of the men were playing a board game with one "English" (i.e. not Amish) woman who had passed by and asked if she could join in. They were clearly having the best time of anyone in the car, laughing loudly with each new move, and bantering back and forth while the Amish women sat separately with their children.

I passed by a fair-haired woman in an apron and head bonnet over a black dress and recognized her as the one who handed out food in the Pittsburgh train station. She held an infant in one arm and sat completely upright, looking straight ahead. It might have been her first child since both she and the man next to her, whom I assumed was her husband, were young. I paused to coo at the baby, who was awake and charming, clothed to the toes in a delicate white smock.

"Your baby is adorable," I said.

The woman glanced down at the child, then up at me. "Thank you."

"How old is she?" I asked.

"It's a boy." Her voice was curt, but I recovered quickly and commented on how practical the gowns like he was wearing were for diaper changing.

"They used to have them in stores all the time when my kids were little, but now you can barely find them," I said, as she shifted her son against her chest.

"I make my own clothes," she said, still stone-faced.

After complimenting her on her sewing abilities, I resumed my mission, blushing with shame. Maybe I thought since the game-playing English woman had broken through and made friends with some of the men, I could chat with the mother about her child, but that was foolish. For part of my adult life, I had lived in Lancaster, Pennsylvania, surrounded by what tourists call "The Aimish." I knew they were very private people who preferred to live peacefully and simply, outside the conventions of government. Their children don't get immunized, nor do they pay taxes—and they don't strike up conversations with strangers.

My way back to the bathroom near my roomette was blocked by a long line of passengers because we were arriving at the first of two Glacier Mountain Park stops in Montana, close to the Canadian border. It's so big (there are 750 miles of trails, over

700 lakes, and 25 glaciers) a special separate train runs through it. Judging from the size of the crowd, it was a popular tourist spot.

Right in front of me was a fit, older gentleman in a stylish parka and scarf behind a boy in a checkered coat and knit cap. Both held small suitcases.

"Are you going to the park?" I asked, not understanding what a big deal that was.

"Yes. We go on a different vacation every summer," he told me and then nodded at his companion. "He's my grandson. Ten years old. That is how old you are, right Sam?"

"Sam" looked shocked for a moment, then realized his grandfather was kidding and bobbed his head up and down.

"One time we went to Disney," Sam said, looking at the older man with the kind of unconditional adoration only a child could offer.

"Yep, we do this every year, pick a vacation and go by ourselves. No parents, right Sam?"

Sam nodded again as the train slowed to a stop. He was so sweet I wanted to ruffle his hair, as I had done with my sons back in the days when Paul and I were fairly new parents full of hope and energy. Instead, I said, "You two must have a lot of fun together. My granddaughter is only three, but maybe someday, we'll do the same thing."

As we pulled up to a quaint log cabin station, I took out my cell phone and turned on the camera, prepared to take a picture after everyone deboarded. A conductor I didn't know stepped between me and the door.

"No pictures," he said.

"Why not?"

"It's a federal park. There's no picture taking allowed."

The rationale didn't make much sense to me, but by then we were pulling out of the station. I could see Sam and his granddad trudging toward what looked like an elegant chalet in the distance. The train traveled for another two hours west before it reached the other way into the park: the Belton West Glacier entrance.

The grandfather and grandson brought a new ache to my heart. The train trip marked my longest separation from my granddaughter, or "granddear," which is my private nickname for her. Her first name for me was the German word for grandmother, "Oma," or something that sounded just like it. Over the years it went through various iterations, including Omay, Omee-Patomee, and finally, she settled on Omee. Paul had been Opa, plain and simple.

By the time our children were old enough to be parents, I thought they would never have children I could enjoy. Due to her eating disorder, we had been told my daughter could never conceive. One of my sons dropped out of college and didn't seem interested in building any kind of traditional life and the other had married a woman with a child he adopted—but they lived on the opposite side of the country, and he was continually traveling for the military. My sister, Beth, had a gaggle of children who lived nearby, and my brother had two daughters in Baltimore, so I contented myself with being "the favorite aunt."

When Joe told me he was planning to get married to his longtime girlfriend, Paul and I had been concerned they were too young. Their relationship had been a rocky one, especially when his wife-to-be had gone away to college for a year, but now they were expecting a baby and committed to staying together.

I have always had a knack for close relationships with young women who enter my life for a time, like the girl Joe intended to marry. Along with her, there had been my Polish exchange student and a medical student whom I refer to as "my protégé" even though she's now an attending physician. Countless high school students who were involved as mentors in my programs for girls became temporary daughters because we collaborated so closely on work we believed to be important. Joe's wife had been my employee for a solid year before the pregnancy, so we had a relationship separate from traditional in-laws that made me hope for the best for them and the baby yet to come.

When they went for their first sonogram, they gave me permission to come along and get a glimpse of my new grandchild. One of my peak life experiences was the image of a walnut sized Granddear fluttering on the—screen—I actually held my breath. I, so already entranced by the little girl who was only a video image, hoped the two of them would be so united by love for their daughter that their marriage would go well.

Although Paul was alive for the first few years of Granddear's life, I ended up spending more time with her, forging the kind of special relationship every grandmother probably claims. After Paul died, she became that kind of consolation to me since we were living in the same house. By the time she was in kindergarten where the teacher directed everyone to draw a picture of their favorite day of the week, Granddear drew a "Wednesday" because that was when I picked her up from school and took her for a swimming lesson.

Instead of beautiful scenery, it was as if my life was playing out on a screen just beyond the window. Grandparenting had been a new aspect to our marriage that I enjoyed, but had Paul? Shortly before Granddear's first birthday, her mother got sick, which made it necessary for someone to provide full-time child care while Joe worked. Since we hoped it would be a short-term arrangement and my job afforded me more flexibility, I promptly transformed an empty bedroom, decorating it with pink curtains, a dresser with flower handles, and lots of stuffed animals.

"Are we really going to be spending that much time with her?" Paul asked on the night when we went out to buy a crib.

"I hope so," I said.

Paul told me he couldn't wait until they were out of the house so he could have me all to himself—a sentiment I didn't share. I loved being a mother and never doubted that he felt the same about fatherhood, but we definitely expressed our feelings differently. Paul's question about how often we would be caring for Granddear had made me realize we never discussed stepping in to help with her—I just assumed we would. Might he have refused?

Even though I was charging forward in real time, it seemed impossible to stop drifting relentlessly to the past—which was not what I intended for the trip. Back in my roomette and slouched on the faux bed, I flipped through the pictures of Granddear on my phone and wondered what she was doing right then. For a moment, I considered calling them, but at her age, she didn't do much more than breathe into the receiver.

It didn't matter. The train route took me in and out of cellphone reception and at that moment I was again cut off from calling with family and friends. In front of me on one end of the convertible bed was my suitcase, open to reveal a pocket full of discarded clothes and a few clean outfits, folded neatly into the bottom, which would see me through the next few days. I zipped it shut and saw the smiling pink face of Hello Kitty again.

At least there were some things in my life that could be counted on to lift my spirits as I imagined Granddear using it in the years to come. I touched the pink vinyl and wished there was a way to imprint it on my heart so I could return to Hershey wearing a happy expression that would see me through the future.

idaho, washington, oregon
the empire builder

Although the route of The Empire Builder cut west until Oregon, I plan to get off in Portland and board The Coast Starlight to travel south to Sacramento, the official halfway point to the trip—at least in my mind. I promised myself that from that moment on, I would only think about things that didn't involve Paul and did involve a new life plan.

After a night of the kind of blessed sleep only exhaustion and powerful medication could produce, I woke in the morning to find that we were charging through a river gorge, a bit like "gorge-ous" Watkins Glen, New York, close to where I grew up. Frequent family trips to Watkins Glen had inspired an appreciation of hiking outdoors, but the view of the Columbia River Gorge was more incredible, even though it was only through a window.

One stretch of clear water tumbled into another in sharp relief against the backdrop of bright blue sky and velvety mountains dappled with gray and brown. When I went to get a cup of water, Mac, the porter, told me the Columbia River Gorge was 55 miles long, formed from water cutting through volcanic ash.

"Why isn't it famous?" I asked, trying to find a good angle to capture the scene on my cellphone camera. The glare of the sun through the scratched windows made it impossible—we were past the best parts by the time I figured that out and gave up.

"It is famous." Mac eyed me as if I was joking and then nodded his head toward the gorge with reverence. "Of all the places I've been in this country, that there is the most beautiful. I never get tired of seeing it." He was an older porter and had somehow replaced Charlie during one of the stops when I was sleeping.

I went to the observation car to be a tourist, hoping there would be more breathtaking scenery, but by then we were beyond gorge territory and the people proved to be more intriguing than the geography. An entirely new crowd of passengers had appeared, more diverse and animated than the ones who had been on board since Chicago.

A few seats away, there was a girl about Granddear's age seated between a man and woman who I presumed to be her parents given the careful way they attended her. The father interested me most since he had a large birthmark across one side of his face, which must have been the first things people noticed about him, and yet his hair was pulled back away from it in a ponytail, and he held his head high. His interactions with the girl and woman were warm and loving, and when he caught me looking at him, he nodded and smiled.

I couldn't help wondering about the man, who probably was treated differently because of the birth defect. He didn't seem to have the defeated attitude that had hung over Paul in the last year of his life. What explained that difference?

"You need to tell your doctor that the antidepressant isn't working," I had suggested at one point, worried by the long periods he would spend on the sofa, silently staring at the television, which was turned off. It was painful to be around him by then, since the only times he seemed remotely happy were when Granddear visited. Nothing I tried would perk him up: a funny movie, a vacation, loving cards, and hugs all seemed not to make a dent in his dark mood. Having experienced depression myself, I knew how painful his inner world was but couldn't find a way to fix it.

After several reminders, Paul did call his physician and was told no other medication would work any better than what he was already on. When I learned more about the kind of alcoholism he had, a therapist friend told me that it was likely he hadn't responded to antidepressants because of his heavy drinking.

"It's the first thing I ask about," she said. "If someone is on a boatload of meds and still not feeling better, booze is usually to blame."

Why hadn't I been more aggressive in encouraging him to get other treatment? Part of me couldn't help blaming his psychiatrist for not probing deeper and figuring out the real problem—but maybe she had. After he died and I went through the painful task of clearing out his belongings, there were so many prescriptions in the medicine cabinet that he used, I was stunned. I hadn't been aware that he was on such big doses of so many meds—or that he stashed them in suit pockets, car ash trays, and dresser drawers.

My reflections were interrupted by a call that somehow made it through the spotty cellphone reception.

"Hey, how's the trip to nowhere going? Is the book written yet?" My sister Beth sounded distracted, but with four kids of assorted ages and their friends running around her house, that wasn't unusual.

"I told you, I'm not writing a book," I said.

"We should write a memoir. It could be called *Bookends* because we're so alike, but then again..." she had a flair for pausing to add the exact right emphasis, "I'm so young and you're so old."

"Watch it, sister, or I'll spill more stories about changing your diapers."

We talked for a while and I tried to describe the Columbia River Gorge to her since she, like me, was a water person—so much that she held her wedding ceremony at Watkins Glenn on a misty rainy Saturday afternoon. Fortunately, the sun had come out after the ceremony when we were celebrating in a nearby picnic area.

Beth had loved Paul in a way none of my other siblings did. Perhaps it was because he took her seriously during her high school years and never teased her about her appearance during the tender adolescent stage when the curves of her body were shifting, unlike other family members. When the two of them went to see *Apocalypse Now* at his suggestion, she became his biggest supporter. While my mother clucked over his shaking hands and my dad continued to tally up how many cans of beer disappeared when he was there, Beth argued that Paul might be a drinker, but he had many redeeming qualities.

The day he died, I called my son, Joe, first and Beth next. They both came immediately, followed by Paul's mother and his younger brother. As we sat close together in the NICU room watching a machine breathe for Paul, my mother-in-law kept encouraging us to call my oldest son, who was stationed in Afghanistan. She didn't seem to accept that I had been trying to call and tell her not to make the trip from the other side of the country, unaware that the Red Cross, alerted by my chaplain colleague, was already in the process of tracking him down and bringing him to Hershey.

"Stop." Finally I frowned at my mother-in-law. "I've already tried calling five times."

"Can I get you some coffee?" my sister asked Paul's mom, deflecting the negativity for a moment.

With all the emotion swirling around the room, Beth somehow had the energy to act as a buffer between my frayed nerves and our deeply shocked family and friends. No matter what she did in the years that followed that might frustrate me, I would always remember those hours and the great gift she gave us all.

It may sound strange but there were other gifts that day. During my growing up years, my family was not particularly affectionate, but as my parents aged they began to greet me with a hug and say, "I love you," each time we were together, which felt like an extreme change of behavior. In the NICU I witnessed a similar transformation as both Paul and my coworkers and acquaintances stepped up to support me in ways I couldn't have imagined. There weren't enough thank you notes to write to capture my gratitude, but each time I sat down to complete the three packages of cards I had bought, it was too overwhelming to actually write anything. That bothered me because people would not know how many little things had meant so much to me. Perhaps someday, some of my comforters will read this and know that when I couldn't formulate thoughts on how people could help or what I needed from others, they gave the best gift intuitively: themselves.

———◆———

I was looking forward to our layover in Portland, the largest city in Oregon, believing there would be a lounge like the one in Chicago. Instead, I spent four hours in a room much like the one in Pittsburgh, only clean and sparsely populated. It was anticlimactic for sure since I had thought I could get to the famous Powell's Bookstore during the layover. There was just enough room to walk around outside the station and keep my luggage in view at all times, so I did some slow jogging around the platform, not caring what I looked like. My marathon and triathlete days were already far behind me when Paul died, but he and I had been swimming regularly and going for long walks from time to time. Those habits died along with Paul and every ounce of energy

I had got diverted to surviving a new life that wasn't especially promising. Who cared if my heart rate and blood pressure were within normal limits?

It felt good to leave the constant rumble of the train and have solid ground beneath me. At one point in American history, "vibration therapy" had been a reputable treatment for various maladies, something I thought about from time to time when traveling by train. Practitioners of the art experimented with precursors of the vibrator applied to various parts of the body in various positions, and some of the time, it worked. Maybe that explained why train travel could feel so relaxing—but getting off reminded me of that moment after roller skating when you walk a few unsteady steps without wheels under your feet.

Tilting my face up to catch the June sunshine, I decided the first improvement I would make when I returned home was to get back into an exercise routine. I always felt better when I swam, my life-long activity that took off in my junior year of high school. There had been a lot of buzz about Title 9 legislation which mandated equal sports opportunities for girls. Since my school had no girls swim team, my best friend, Nancy, and I decided to try out for the boys' team. As dedicated AAU swimmers, we both qualified for and competed on the boys' team for one year, after which the school launched a girls' program.

It was perhaps the most formative year of my life since I learned an early lesson on sexism. There were parents who protested and others who wrote newspaper articles about the disgrace of girls competing against boys and potentially "taking away" something from the boys. Thankfully I had Nancy and her mother beside me to make the long walk to and from the Girls Locker Room after swim meets, but more than once there were catcalls and negative comments about our presence.

While I think our coach didn't quite know what to make of being forced to allow girls on the team, there were some who cheered us on. For me, surviving practice and finishing my races was the best I could hope for, but Nancy was strong enough to take second place in some of the meets, which caused applause but no small amount of resentment. She and I were both considered heroines by most of the girls in our class, but the boys tended toward suspicion and sarcasm, especially the ones who came in third in Nancy's races.

That was a memory that always made me feel good: overcoming the odds on the Boys Swim Team and going on to be the founding member and co-captain of the first Girls Swim Team. Yes, swimming was perfect—as soon as I returned home, I would start doing laps again. At least I would be putting my energy toward something healthy.

It's good you've learned something, but isn't traveling across the country just to discover you need to work out more a bit extreme? You're almost at the halfway point, you know. Shouldn't there be some bigger insight?

The snarky voice had a way of confirming the other not-so-uplifting thoughts that flitted through my mind as I drew closer to the time when I would be going back toward rather than away from Hershey.

Each accusation from the darker part of my brain was like a stark black bird that soared up against a faded blue sky.

—*You've spent a small fortune on this trip, and it's hardly been worth it.*

—*Seems like all this reminiscing is making things worse, instead of better.*

—*Is any of this going to help you in any way rebuild your life in Hershey?*

—*Don't forget, you and Jack are finished, too. Are you really going to go back on Match.com and start all over with someone else?*

In my clinical work, I had heard so many widows glorify their husbands, remembering the quick laugh but not the bad temper, or the loving parent instead of the neglectful husband. I, on the other hand, felt fixated on my discovery of how very sick Paul was during his lifetime. At first, discovering the unpaid taxes and pills tucked into pockets of his suits and trousers made me furious with myself for being so naive.

How could you possibly play innocent? There were plenty of signs there for you to see, my critic reminded me, and correctly so. There were so many red flags I should have stopped believing his denial. Like the time he left a gas station with the fuel hose still attached to his car—it wasn't just "forgetfulness."

At the time, we actually laughed about it and referred to him as "the absentminded professor" because he was a man whose boss described him as "scary smart" and the "go-to guy for difficult cases." Could anyone like that be a serious alcoholic?

More importantly, when would all my book knowledge about grief prove to be true? A few years after I stopped teaching Death and Dying, psychologists, Alexander Jordan and Brett Litz, proposed several behaviors that indicated "Prolonged Grief Disorder," and at that point in my trip, I met most of them. There was daily yearning for the deceased, bitterness or anger related to the loss, emotional numbness since the loss, a feeling of being stunned or dazed and the criteria: "At least six months have passed since the death." What did it say about me, an expert on death and dying, being completely miserable in twice that amount of time? Recently, the addition of a diagnostic category was proposed to capture prolonged or profound grief.

A little girl at the Portland station came onto the platform with her family, making me think of Granddear. Although I had always thought I loved her more than Paul did, after he died, one of his other secrets was revealed: he had started a college savings account for her without telling me. In contrast to the other things I discovered, it was a pleasant surprise.

I smiled at the child and gave her a tiny wave as our train prepared to board.

oregon, california
the coast starlight

To my disappointment, The Coast Starlight ran from Seattle to Los Angeles far enough inland to prevent any view of the coast or ocean. When I had seen pictures of the route online, I thought it might recreate a trip Paul and I had taken to California two years before he died. I attended a medical conference in San Francisco and he came along because our children were out of the house by then, making it a smaller version of the Sweden experience. Removed from the pressures of his work and daily life in Hershey, I saw a different side of him.

"Let's drive to Malibu," he suggested, wanting to travel on Highway One near the ocean and check out a place he vaguely remembered from childhood when his father had been stationed in San Diego. As a Gidget fan, I wanted to see beaches like the ones she and her friends surfed in, so I readily agreed. Our mood was light when we took off, map in hand, deciding we would drive as far as we could in one afternoon and evening.

Nearly six hours later, we stopped at Malibu and kicked off our shoes off to wriggle our toes in the sand at the edge of the only part of the famous beach we could access. The sun was setting over the ocean, so we hunched in silence, watching the scene before grabbing dinner at a shockingly expensive restaurant. Wanting to walk a bit before we climbed back in the car and returned to San Francisco, we poked around the little shops that were still open.

"I love that art," I said, stopping in front of a small place with impressionist style paintings in the window.

"Go on in," he said, and so we did, impressed as an elegantly clad woman approached us and began pointing out pieces we might like. I studied one that reminded me a bit of Mark's angel art with an abstract mix of bright colors. Most of the pictures on our walls came from places where Paul's parents had traveled or were gifts from well-off friends. When a realtor had come to appraise our house one time, he commented to his partner, "This is the place with the interesting art," which surprised me given the randomness of our selections.

"How much is this?" I finally asked the woman, who was gazing at the painting just as intently as I was.

"100," she said. It took me a moment to realize she meant $100,000, not $100 and it was all I could do not to drop it as if it was a bee that had stung me.

"Let's keep looking," Paul said, but after the dinner and the casual way money was referred to, we shook our heads in shock once we got to the privacy of the rental car. It was hard to reconcile that Paul, amused by the difference between the Malibu he remembered and the current Malibu that was clearly a different economic stratum than ours, was the same person who would have a dark cloud of depression surrounding him a year later.

That was what I thought of as I fell asleep on the southbound train that twisted through northern California. The trip wasn't going to be long—we were expected in Sacramento at 6:35 a.m., so I wanted to rest up—but it seemed like I had barely dozed off, remembering that fun day, when a conductor woke us.

"Rise and shine, we're almost there," she said, sounding remarkably like the person who cautioned against late boarding in Oregon, assuring us, "If you aren't on the train, we aren't waiting for you."

Except that now it was 5 a.m. and her voice was strident as she went down the sleeper car's hall, banging on the door of every roomette. Along with a crowd of other sleepy passengers, I gathered my belongings and was herded into the midst of what appeared to be the morning commute. People were bustling in and out of the large open-air building that formed the Sacramento station, wide-awake despite the early hour and intent on boarding whatever train they were taking to work. There were no signs indicating the way to the waiting room.

When I approached a gentleman behind a counter with the Amtrak logo on it and asked where it might be, he laughed.

"You're standing in it," he said, and before I could ask any further questions, he shook his head "no," pulled on his coat, and marched away, saying over his shoulder, "My shift is finished."

It was the first time I had to manage my bigger Hello Kitty suitcase, which had grown heavy with books and pamphlets about the train acquired at various station stores along the way. Previously, the porters were more than happy to hoist it around, and I was more than happy to tip them generously for it, but once we exited the train, I was on my own.

Somehow, I inched over to one of the curve-backed wooden benches and sat down, wrapping my arms around my body in an attempt to keep warm. How could California be so cold in June?

There was a tiny newsstand inside the station where I bought a watery cup of hot chocolate that temporarily warmed me, but after the early rush of commuters, the stucco building was nearly empty. It was a shock to realize this train station in the capital of California, open to the elements, was little more than a big room with benches.

On the lawn outside, dozens of homeless people still slept, wrapped in sleeping bags. I later learned that the "unsheltered" population in Sacramento was so large, one activist suggested reserving a dedicated space for them in the city. Like in Harrisburg, many of those without a safe and secure place to live were mentally ill, victims of domestic violence, or part of a homeless family. My volunteer work informed me of the many forms of homelessness; couch surfing, sleeping in a car, living on the streets, or "staying with friends," were just a few examples of a lifestyle where every day is a struggle for food and shelter.

Birds swooped in and out the waiting room, snapping up scraps of food. Four other passengers from The Coast Starlight drifted over to me. We introduced ourselves and exchanged complaints about being ejected from the train early, then ranted about the cold temperature and uncomfortable seats we were forced to endure. One neatly groomed passenger, dressed in Birkenstocks and creased khaki shorts, held a Styrofoam container in his right hand, watching as a bedraggled man approached the flock of people spread out on the grass.

"Hey guys, it's all-you-can-eat pancake day at Perkins," the unkempt man announced. For some reason, the fellow passenger standing with us took this as a signal to approach the group with his box.

"Hi there!" he said, holding the container toward the customer from Perkins. "I have some cake left over from the train and hate to waste it. Would you like it?"

Everyone froze at the body language and expression of the shaggy young man who had come to share his breakfast bounty with people who clearly knew him.

"No. Thanks." He gave the passenger guy a fierce look and took a menacing step toward him. "I just paid for a big breakfast at Perkins."

I closed my eyes in a silent prayer, understanding what an insult the well-intended passenger had just delivered. The tense scene ended when he dumped his cake box in the trashcan, mumbled an apology, and sauntered back to the rest of us.

We moved ever so slightly away from him so the offended guy would know we did not sanction the offering of unwanted cake. I sat alone until I was shaking with cold.

"Would you mind watching my bags while I walk around a little?" I asked one of the other women, who was dressed warmly.

"Sure. My husband is going to look around too," she said, swinging her legs up sideways on the wooden seat and leaning back on a suitcase. "And I'm going to take a little snooze; I can sleep anywhere, but don't worry, I'll wake up if anyone touches our stuff."

As I moved through the city blocks nearest to the train station, which were part of Old Sacramento, the temperature started to rise, and the chill evaporated. By the time I had trudged around for half an hour, the neighborhood was waking up and people were trickling out of a combination of sharp angled new business buildings alongside more traditional stucco style houses. In the middle of a park, a group of older Asian American women did Tai chi, their movements so precise they seemed choreographed for a commercial about healthy aging.

I discovered the Sacramento River, the largest river in California which eventually empties in the San Francisco Bay. Perhaps because one of its tributaries started the Gold Rush, there were souvenir stores near the river walkway, offering the same kind of trinkets as the beach towns where I had vacationed back at home: bags of fake gold, painted felt banners, and snow globes with replicas of the pony express inside. A luxury riverboat hotel, The Delta King, was anchored within view of a promenade that led me back to the train station, where the sun was now shining brightly. The group of people who had been sprawled outside there an hour before were nowhere in sight.

It was hard to believe Sacramento had been a charter city and site of the country's first transcontinental railroad, as well located close to Sutter's Mill, where the first gold rush appeared. My previous trips to San Francisco, San Diego, and Los Angeles had imprinted an image of California in my mind's eye: sunshine and modern architecture, with the kind of glamor New York City possesses only in summer pastels instead of black. Now I was seeing a city where the homeless population wasn't hidden away in parks or under bridges but camped outside a major transportation hub.

Nonetheless, it was my turnaround point and I was suddenly cheered by that thought. Back to the East, and my new life.

california, nevada, utah, colorado
the california zephyr

It was nearly noon when we boarded The California Zephyr. I climbed up the steps to my roomette, feeling the steady but slight vibration of the engine through the floor and being comforted by the constant sensation.

We would head northeast through Nevada, then Utah, and on to Colorado as we made our way back up to Chicago. The scenery on this part of the trip was supposed to be fabulous, but as soon as we hit the desert, I turned away from the window. Although we were not going through Arizona, the landscape reminded me too much of the many trips I had made there. For several years I had been a frequent flier in and out of Phoenix and spent my vacation days visiting my daughter in various facilities a good distance from the airport. It was a state that somehow attracted any number of residential treatment centers for girls with eating disorders or other addictions.

The first time we flew to Arizona, I had high hopes. My daughter was sixteen and had been in and out of hospitals that took her further and further from home for the previous two years. When she was remanded (i.e. court ordered) to a pediatric hospital outside of Philadelphia, I despaired, but at least she would still be in the state of Pennsylvania.

Although it was a bright and fairly new facility only two hours away, I felt nauseated every time I went there to visit. How could my daughter be locked so far away from me? The patients were so different from the young women she had been surrounded by in her previous treatments. Many were violent, constantly striking out at staff or each other; one time my daughter got beat up by another girl before the attendants could separate them.

"No one likes her," a chubby social worker told me when we met in person for the first time. "Your daughter is very difficult."

As we sat face to face in her tiny office, our knees nearly touching, I held up a hand to halt the tirade. "Wait. That's my child you're talking about. I don't care at all if you like her—I love her and it's your job to help her, not put her down."

It was clear I needed to get Ellen out of there, but the only way to do so with a court order was to transfer her to another facility. With several pages of information in hand, I appealed to the lead psychiatrist to release her to Arizona where the premier treatment facility in the country was located. On the telephone, I was assured they had the best likelihood of helping my daughter.

While she wouldn't have gone there voluntarily since she wasn't ready to give up her eating disorder, when the psychiatrist offered her an option to be transferred out of the psychiatric hospital, she took it. On the long plane trip to Phoenix, my stomach had churned at the thought of dropping her on the other side of the country without my ready comfort and perseverance to sustain her. Little did I know this would be a repeating theme throughout her illness—more and more space between us, first just one locked door and then more, and then an entire locked facility, and finally prison. Each new barrier made me feel I lost a little more of her.

On the train, we passed Reno, transformed into the "biggest little city in the world" due to gold mining, casino gambling, and liberal divorce laws. I pawed through my backpack for the medication bag I carried everywhere. I rarely took the daytime sedatives that got me through the first six months after Paul died but had saved a few for those "just in case" situations. Nevada had become one of them, tears pricking at my eyes. I snapped a white pill in half and popped it in my mouth as we pushed past miles of sandy landscape that mirrored the Arizona geography I had driven through for hours to reach the treatment facility that first time. Just beyond the windows of The California Zephyr, spidery trails snaked to and from little towns where there wasn't much more than scattered ranches and farms converted to facilities offering hope for hopeless cases. I pulled the curtain shut and closed my eyes as the medication began to work, thankful for chemicals that allowed me to escape reality for a few hours.

I roused enough to go to dinner where I was sandwiched at a table, family style, with four tall people headed to Salt Lake City.

"We're Mormons, of course," the mother/spokesperson explained after informing me of their destination. "That's where we're from."

She was a soft woman with sandy blonde hair and a bit of extra weight, while her husband was tall and thin, reminding me or the "Jack Spratt" nursery rhyme. The two other adults were their son and daughter, along for a trip no one described any further.

The professional side of me wondered about the older man, whose pasty complexion, flat affect, and slight frame suggested illness. When our meals arrived, the woman cut some of his food into tiny bites and scraped the rest onto her plate.

Normally, I would work harder at a conversation with them, but I was still a bit drowsy, and their demeanor was so reserved it seemed best to eat quickly and return to my roomette. Once there, I settled into my seat and eased the curtain back open. There was a gray dusk settling over the rocky terrain with a border of skyscraper mountains in the distance, I decided it was a good time to take my regular sleeping pill and call it a day.

As I drifted off to sleep, it occurred to me that my anger at Paul's addictions was a bit misplaced. Since his death, I had become dependent on prescriptions to calm me down, cheer me up, and put me to sleep.

"I think it might be time to try a taper," my physician suggested as the one-year anniversary approached. "I'm concerned with how much you're taking."

"I will, once I get back from my trip," I said to appease her. Secretly I had no intention of stopping anything.

It had become my habit to reach for a pill the first thing each morning—maybe just one pill, but nonetheless a drug that got me out of bed and able to face the day. They were like gems, guarded in my purse and always with me at work or wherever else I happened to go. Each time I packed up to deboard the train, I made sure they were easily accessible.

I justified the medicine as a "temporary" fix, not a permanent solution in the way Paul had. Unhealthy, yes, but justifiable given the craziness of my past year. Gazing out the window at the scenery, which had become as stellar as the Amtrak literature suggested it would be, I found myself thinking in terms somewhat between a promise and a prayer.

I can do better, I thought. *And I'll be more understanding of what Paul went through... he probably thought his drinking and drugging weren't a long-term solution, too.* For a change, it was my own voice that was chiding, not the harsh judgmental one that had haunted me throughout the first part of my trip.

———◆———

Life had become a prayer the instant I saw Paul sprawled on the basement floor, and throughout the last year, God was there on my journey. That was different from "religion," which dictated so many practices surrounding death.

Sure, I went to church every Sunday as was my habit and spoke about faith and turned to clergy for help, but what buoyed me up the most was a realization that came during my worst moments. God was always there, so gentle in the day-to-day struggles it was easy to take for granted. It was in the times of darkest despair, however, that I felt Him most forcefully, almost a physical support that kept me upright and moving forward.

As per his wishes, Paul was cremated. Although I had a viewing, and a day later a memorial service, finding a cemetery and headstone for yet one more gathering (a formal burial) was beyond me. Also, I wasn't ready to remove the burnished wooden box containing his ashes from its place next to my bed.

A few days after he died, I created a memorial altar and positioned it next to the side of the bed where he had slept. Something I read suggested this sort of thing could be a helpful activity for those who had suffered a loss, and for me, it was. Although I switched items from time to time, the religious artifacts and candles remained.

Paul, who was raised as a devout Catholic by his father, left church behind when he went to college but agreed it was important for our family to attend together. Since I was a devout Lutheran, we went with that. Still, he was the one to insist the priest come and give his father last rites, a ritual he asked me to guarantee for him if he predeceased me.

Even though he had only attended our local Catholic church on rare occasions when I prompted it (midnight Christmas mass), I complied. The parish priest who showed up was clearly disappointed when I couldn't tell him that Paul was an active member of the church, but that didn't matter to me. On a spiritual level, I had done my best.

The train was climbing higher and higher as we left Salt Lake City and headed for Provo, home of the famous singing Osmond siblings. At one point, I glanced down from my window and realized the rail track was, at best, a few yards from the edge of sheer cliff. By the time we reached Soldier Summit, a Utah landmark where Civil War soldiers were buried, we were at 7000 feet, but headed back down to Green River, the lowest point between Salt Lake City and Denver. Somehow I managed to sleep, although my final thoughts were of the precipice just beyond my window.

———◆———

The next day I found myself seated at lunch with a woman and her two sons who chattered to each other in French. When the meal was served, the younger boy complained about the food, and I couldn't refrain from smiling.

"Je parle francais aussi," I said, surprised that my graduate school review of the language had stayed with me.

The mother, who introduced herself as Anne, laughed and said to her son, "Go ahead, talk to her. She can understand you."

We ended up speaking in English for the rest of the meal and on occasion when we passed each other in the hallway thereafter. She was the real deal—born and raised in France but teaching the language at a Midwestern college when she met her husband. They married, he finished his PhD, and the two of them moved to California where he could pursue a career and they could have their children.

"My dad is going to discover the cure for cancer," the older boy told me proudly, looking at his mother for affirmation. Anne smiled and nodded.

As part of a faculty of physicians and researchers, I found their claim curious. If there was ever a "cure for cancer," it seemed clear no one person would happen upon it in isolation—there would be years of preliminary study that would lead to important break-throughs—but I didn't share that thought with Anne or her sons. Clearly, their family revolved around the missing father, who had stayed behind to finish up an "important work project."

Later, when we hit a rest stop, Anne ran laps back and forth at the station while her oldest son sat with a stopwatch at the window of their roomette, nodding at her each time she passed back and forth. Walking parallel to her, I wished my body would still permit me to run.

Anne and her young sons were headed for a famous luxury resort at Glenwood Springs, where there were six world-class ski resorts, whitewater rafting, and miles of bike trails. Seeing them get off the train together (her boys carrying the suitcases so she wouldn't have to) was a tender and touching scene.

Like just about every woman who crossed my path in the year after Paul died, Anne seemed to have the perfect family and perfect life: slender and attractive with a successful husband, charming children, and a carefully organized lifestyle that included very little television, healthy cooking, and the opportunity to run and read at her leisure.

She was young and married. I was old and widowed. She had two sons who adored her and a husband who was taking the family on a posh vacation. I had children in a perpetual state of crisis and a husband who was never coming back into my life.

Stop, I told myself. *If you want to change your life, you can't keep comparing yourself to women whose situations are nothing like yours. Find some other people to connect with if you really want to play that game.*

Little did I know that I soon would.

new mexico to chicago
the california zephyr

By the time we left Glenwood Springs, I felt a pounding that signaled a high-altitude headache, something I experienced once while at a conference in New Mexico. Before long, it felt like my brain was being sawed in half. The train's swaying added to my agony so that I couldn't even laugh when a group of young people riding down what must have been the Colorado River flipped over and mooned the train as we passed. The view from the train window was beautiful, but my head continued to throb even with a dose of my migraine medication from the rainbow mix of pills I carried everywhere.

Finding the right one, I stood up to go for a cup of the ice water available at the porter's station, a bit dizzy.

"Are you okay?" a voice asked.

A bit foggy from the pain clamping down on my head, I looked across the aisle and found that the person in the cubicle across from mine had her curtains halfway drawn. A woman peered out around them; I vaguely remembered her coming and going to the last meal, but she had stayed inside her roomette otherwise, which I assumed meant she wanted privacy.

Now, a pair of bright brown eyes peered out at me, concerned.

"No," I groaned. "I have a terrible headache."

"Oh, there's another person upstairs who's really sick, too. She's traveling with a 90-year-old woman who's sleeping up top—can you imagine?" The woman tilted her head and smiled, her face relaxing into wrinkle patterns that suggested a happy life.

"Up top," the narrow ledge above each compartment meant to provide a bunk bed option. I already knew it would take a very nimble person to climb up there and insert him or herself in the "bed," so the idea of a 90-year-old doing it made me smile briefly in spite of my misery.

"Good for her. I hope I can be that flexible when I'm ninety."

I stumbled to the steps where the glass container of water waited, popped in my medicine, and swallowed hard. How could I continue with the trip when my head was pounding so violently it seemed I was on the verge of a stroke?

Paul was the only person who understood my migraines, although he rarely had headaches or any other illness. On our honeymoon, I got a terrible one and ended up in bed for an entire day. He had been there to check on me and run to the store for ginger ale or special food that I needed, and through the years that followed when the pattern repeated itself, he made sure to keep the children quiet while I was laid low by the thunderstorm in my brain. Although I had my first migraine in third grade, sometimes I wondered if their frequency was a consequence of the competing demands crammed into my life.

"Why do you have to do so many things?" he asked me once, as I packed up my bags for a week-long writing conference. At the time, I thought he just didn't realize how important that part of my life was, but as the train swayed from side to side on the steep Colorado tracks, I wondered if my constant activity was not only the cause of headaches but also a reason for his drinking.

From the moment we married, Paul's mother, Marie, had joined my own mother criticizing my desire to "have a career." Both made negative comments about my hectic lifestyle, which was so unlike their own. After Paul died, his mother made attempts to be kind, but when I found out she told my children that my lifestyle was the cause of Paul's fall and subsequent death, it fractured our relationship for good.

I gulped down several cups of water and made my way back to the roomette, hands against the walls of the hallway for support as I walked. The fluid in my stomach added a feeling of nausea to my discomfort.

"By the way, I'm Esther. I've been trying to catch your eye and introduce myself," my pixie-like neighbor said when I arrived back at my spot. "But I thought maybe you wanted to be left alone."

I introduced myself and asked where she was headed, hoping a conversation might distract me.

"I live outside of Chicago. I was just visiting my sister, who's had some terrible bad luck. This is the first time I've gone on the train. How about you?"

"Oh, I'm running away from home," I said, my voice lighter than I felt. "I'm a veteran train rider, but not across the country, like this."

"Across the country? What would make you take a trip like that?"

"An adventure, I guess."

It turned out that Esther was fifteen years older than me, but something about her suggested youth and energy. Perhaps it was her quick smile or the way she spoke, with a bit of a lilt that suggested a good sense of humor. Our exchange deepened when we discovered we were both nurses, mothers of struggling adult children, and widowed.

She had married her high school sweetheart, John, and raised a family with him before he got sick. Then she watched him die of cancer, slowly and surely, over the course of several years. Still, memories of even the last days they spent together made her smile rather than frown.

"One time we went on a picnic. I loaded him up with all of his equipment, the oxygen and the feeding tube and the catheter, and off we went to the park. It was a real adventure. Thank goodness I'm a nurse. I don't know how we would have done it otherwise. All those years of him being so ill."

When John's last days came, she told me, they were both ready. "It couldn't have ended any better. We both were at peace with him passing."

The chunk of grief lodged inside me shifted for a moment. How could she be so content after losing John and having her grown children and one grandchild move back in with her because they "fell apart" when he died?

"I wish I could feel that way," I said, fidgeting with my cellphone, which still had no reception. "'At peace' with things."

"Ah, but that's the other part of dying—what happens after as much as what leads up to it."

My headache had eased by the time we closed our curtains and settled into our made-up beds for the night, but the next morning, after breakfast, Esther and I picked up where we had left off, skipping from subject to subject like old friends reunited after years apart. Like time travelers passing through different eras, we continued eastward. As we crossed from Iowa into Illinois and rode over miles of the Mississippi that were a mix of slick mud and water, we compared our schools, our childhoods, our jobs, our children, and then again, our grief.

There was no regret or bitterness in her voice when she spoke about her life—and she never sought another partner after John died. We continued to exchange parts of our stories for a long time, saying things only two women with medical backgrounds and a measure of brokenness could share.

In the world of academe and health care, death is a one size fits all concept. Parents who have lost a child, widows young and old, and teenagers whose friends committed suicide were all considered to go through the same grieving process. I was just as guilty as the other experts who referred to death and dying in terms that suggested personal details didn't alter the process.

"Does it ever get easier?" I asked. "It's been a year and I'm still so sad."

"I don't know that it's easy, but it's tolerable." Esther tilted her head and looked at me, silent for a second. "You get used to it, maybe."

Had she been better prepared to cope than me? With each surgery that cut away bits of her husband, she mourned, noting that it seemed like a new piece of equipment got added for each part removed, a specter of what was to come. Eventually, the pain was agonizing for both of them, and although I didn't ask, I knew from my clinical work that spouses sometimes prayed for death so their loved ones' suffering would end.

If the mass on Paul's kidney had been discovered sooner and turned out to be cancer, I might have had to watch him suffer, perhaps for years. Was that better than discovering, too late, that he had been in a state of torment for most of our marriage, resorting to alcohol and drugs to numb the pain? Was his suffering, distilled over many adult years, any easier than John's?

The train streaked across acres of farmland turned golden in the afternoon sun and then slowed as dabs of little towns peppered the landscape, first sparse and then closer, like pop beads on a necklace. At the crossings, each community was like a Xeroxed copy of the one before, advertisements for rural America at its best. There were businessmen with ties loosened, children straddling bikes, and women in jeans clustered behind the yellow arm of the train guard, their crossing interrupted by our passage.

Beyond the towns, farm equipment moved across the fields like metal monsters, not far from houses with barns and rope washing lines flagged with clothing. Every now and then, I'd catch sight of a little kid waving frantically at the train, prompting the conductor to give a "hello" toot back with the horn.

As Esther's suburban Chicago stop neared, we exchanged email addresses, although she told me she wasn't "a fan of the computer." I realized that most likely, we would never correspond. As she zipped up her handbag and prepared for her stop, I felt a pang of sadness.

"Thank you," I said.

"Goodness, for what?"

"Just for talking. For sharing all that stuff."

She was positioning her purse over one shoulder and angling the rolling suitcase that was about as tall as her into place but stopped at my comment. Her eyes were soft as she looked at me.

"We have a lot in common. That's how I know you're going to be fine," she said, with a wink.

Then she was gone.

chicago, illinois, indiana, ohio, pennsylvania
the capitol limited

The second time around, the lounge in the Chicago train station didn't seem so special, even though it was still by far the nicest one I had encountered on my trip. As I waited for the first train in the final leg of my travels eastward, I sifted back through the information Esther had shared, thinking it must contain hidden clues about how to deal with death.

Sitting in the luxurious Chicago train station, instead of feeling angry or raging over the meaninglessness of Paul's death, I realized that a big part of my sadness related to the waste of his life and the loss of our future. Like the spy, Eddie Chapman, Paul had been brilliant at deception, but I was a nurse as well as his wife. I should have been able to see the hidden symptoms of his disease and address the pain that caused it. For the first time, grief felt like a tragedy instead of an attack, and I understood what so many who have lost a loved one tried to explain to me: the bereaved lose a life as well. We are no longer a partner or a friend or a child; we're left behind to learn a new role. I was a widow instead of a wife, and not a parent but *the* parent.

If only I had known these things when I stood in front of the classroom and tried to share the copious readings I had done on death and dying with my students. How many of them were out there in the world believing, as I once did, that after a year life returned to baseline and you went on living as you had before your loved one vanished in every way but the memories?

———————

Previously, a porter had been waiting to direct passengers toward the sleeper cars, but for some reason, that didn't happen when I boarded The Capitol Limited in Chicago. Figuring that either Don, the travel agent, had made a mistake or I somehow lost the special sleeper ticket, I headed for the regular car. There were only a few seats left, so I grabbed the nearest one on an aisle, heaved my Hello Kitty suitcase onto the overhead rack, and arranged my backpack and purse beneath me.

Since I entered nursing school at age 17 and had to start rising at 6 a.m. to be on the floor for clinical, both my best friend, Susan, and I fretted about sleep. It was especially bad on Sunday nights after a weekend of partying in our own modest way. Since we were the two students whose families lived several hours from campus, we had a routine for each day: Friday and Saturday nights were fraternity parties and Sunday nights were spent trolling the grounds of Franklin & Marshall College to see if any of the guys we had met that weekend were hanging around. That was usually a disappointing process, made worse by the realization that our routine of studying and clinicals would soon resume.

"I can't believe the weekend is over," I would start, when we headed back to our dorm after it turned too dark to see much or we had given up on any sightings.

"What time is it?" she would ask and then, after checking our watches, we would both groan.

"It's nine o'clock, Susan. Even if we iron our uniforms and polish our shoes and get our showers and go right to bed, we'll still only get…seven hours."

"That's if we fall right asleep," she would add, knowing that neither of us would have such luck. In our dormitory back in the mid-1970s, Sunday nights were a mad rush among the students to use the two ironing boards available; organize pens, bandage scissors, and name pins; make sure our shoes were shiny white without any scuff or other marks; and finally, to find a pair of white stockings without runs. By the time all these activities were completed, Susan's and my mind had kicked into such high gear there was no hope of falling asleep quickly.

As the clock crept closer to the magic hour of six a.m., the sense of panic over too little sleep and too much work in the day ahead would escalate. The cycle repeated every week because it never occurred to us that we might spend Saturdays preparing our uniforms and polishing our shoes when we had the dorm to ourselves.

As I boarded the train and prepared to depart from Chicago, that same anxiety bubbled up in me. My trip was in its final stages and soon I would return to my "real" life, but in that moment my bigger concern was how I would manage to get any rest in a regular train seat during the last night of my trip? How did I fail to book a sleeper? Did I have enough medicine to knock myself out? It was one thing to doze during a short trip but spending a night in the upright seats with no pillow to cushion the spine I had surgically repaired shortly before Granddear was born would be impossible.

In the seat in front of me, a couple with their arms entwined exchanged quick kisses and laughs.

"Excuse me," the girl said to the conductor who happened to be walking down the aisle, a short, round woman in the blue Amtrak uniform and a sharply creased, fresh white shirt. "Could you check and see if there are any sleepers? This is our honeymoon, and we thought...well...anyway, if there's one available, we'd like it."

The conductress smiled broadly. "I got you."

She wrote down their names on a small notepad she took from her pocket. When she was done, I lifted my hand in a half wave.

"Excuse me? I'd like to be on the list for a sleeper, too."

She frowned at me. "Didn't you just hear them ask? If there are any at all, they got in line first."

The couple turned to listen to our conversation, exchanging a look with each other, and then the conductor. I shrank down in my seat and checked for email on my newly restored cellphone service.

A few minutes later, the same woman came chugging back through the car, a pad of paper in her hand. "Cheryl Dellasega? Cheryl, are you in this car?"

"That's me," I said.

"Let me see your ticket." She halted next to my seat, one hand on her hip and her eyes fixed on the tablet she held. When I handed it to her, she studied it and then gave me a hard look.

"You're supposed to be in the sleeper car. Get your stuff together and go out and around. They're waiting for you."

The eyes of the honeymooners bored into me as I eased my suitcase from the rack and departed, wondering if maybe I should be nice and offer them my spot. Had they been a little less barbed in the looks they shot at me over the seatbacks and a little more discrete in the way they rolled their eyes at the conductor, maybe I would have considered it.

You need to start looking out for yourself, the voice said, and I hesitated for a split second in shock. That was absolutely right—I did need to start doing what was best for Cheryl, a task that defeated me every time I had considered it in the past. Paul would want me to do well without him.

When I got to the roomette, the porter waiting for me was young and perky. She was wearing long fake nails and her face had a genuine smile on it.

"Wow, I was wondering if you missed the train," she said, grinning. "It's a good thing I'm persistent. I had to ask that conductor two times to go and find you."

With those words, she earned every penny of the generous tip I would give her when I left the train. She flipped the mattress into place with an expert twist of her hands, patted the blanket down and ushered me in.

"You get the prize. Out of all the porters I've had during my trip, no one could manage that with those nails," I said.

She shrugged. "Oh, I'm used to it. I've been doing this job for a couple of years."

She lingered a bit to tell me that, like the other porters, she worked several long days in a row and then returned home to her young children. Somehow, she had enough energy to keep a bustle to her work that probably made her a favorite with passengers.

When she left, she said over her shoulder, "Hey, make sure everything is strapped down. We have a wild engineer tonight who's jumped the tracks before."

It didn't feel like there was any abnormal swaying that night, but I might have been so focused on other things that it escaped my notice. Drifting off to sleep, I remembered that had my original plan worked out, I would have taken a route that led from Sacramento to Louisiana and then straight up along the Mississippi to Chicago on The City of New Orleans (the same as the song). There would still be plenty of time to avoid returning to Hershey if I did that, but my travel buddy, Don, told me that it was next to impossible to book a trip on the CNO. When I called just before departing Harrisburg to see if anything had opened up.

"Since Hurricane Katrina, everybody wants to go and take a look," he explained.

That could be my next trip. For now, I felt I had accomplished my mission. I was ready to see my Lacey, whose little tail would wag so hard her hips wiggled. Her mouth would turn up in a smile the instant she saw me and for the rest of the day, she would stay close, as if making sure I wasn't leaving again.

I would also get back the creature comforts I hadn't appreciated before: TV, the newspaper, cellphone reception, a big bed, and the ability to take a long bath if I felt like it. Best of all, I would be able to grab Granddear and smother her with hugs she would pretend to try to escape even though she loved them.

During one of the stints when Paul attended Alcoholics Anonymous, he told me a common bit of advice from the AA Handbook was "fake it until you make it." In other words, act like you're recovered and eventually you will be—or at least that's how I interpreted it. It suddenly seemed like a good philosophy, and if it worked for those who struggled to resist addiction, it could work for me.

The next morning as we cruised into Pittsburgh, I took inventory using the Amtrak magazine stored in my backpack. It looked like the route I had taken was just about the longest possible East-West stretch of train track across the United States, beginning in Harrisburg and going northwest to Portland, dropping down to Sacramento, California, and then heading back east via Chicago. If I had started from Philadelphia or New York, it would have added some extra miles, and certainly deviating to the south for a pass at Louisiana would have stretched my journey out even further but living on the train for two weeks had been enough. I had showered, eaten, and slept while moving, no longer wobbling when I walked down the aisle when we rounded a curve.

Aside from a few calls to Beth and a friend in Harrisburg, my socialization had been with people on the train: mothers and their children, Lee, Esther, and a few other random casual conversations over a beer in the café or as I sat in front of my laptop in the Observation Car. I wrote remarkably little, even though I had intended to keep a log of the trip.

Only Esther had given me something subtle but important: a goal to strive for. Maybe someday, I would be able to think about

Paul and remember mostly the good times instead of the horrible way he died and the mess that followed. Maybe. In the meantime, I would start crossing items off the new list I had compiled: 1) Start swimming again, 2) Get an appraisal on the house, and 3) Think about starting a journal to describe this experience.

After I boarded The Daily Pennsylvanian, my final train, I called Beth.

"Hey, I'm on my way home," I said.

"So, did you write a book about your trip?" she asked.

"No, but I did write about Paul. I have about fifty pages of really profound thoughts like: 'We met through our mutual best friends.' Then there's the really spicy parts, like the time we took Matt to the pizza restaurant and Paul held him up to watch the cook throw dough up in the air. Is that stuff really important?"

"Maybe it's what he wants you to remember," she said. Typical.

In the background, her children were fighting over who would command the television next. Beth had two teenagers from her first marriage and was now starting again with a younger son and daughter from the second one. They bracketed Granddear in age nicely, so that was another reason we saw each other frequently. I made a mental note to add "See Beth more often" to my list of activities for the future.

I heard her microwave door open, then slam shut, as my niece and nephew escalated into all-out-combat mode in the background.

"Mom! He's hogging the remote. Tell him to stop."

"I am not going to survive this day," she said to me, and then added in the same tone of voice, "Kids, I'm on the phone."

It was doubtful they heard it, since the sounds of small bodies wrestling and being knocked into furniture continued.

"Well, I know you're into all that spiritual stuff, but I was hoping for an epiphany, not some message from Paul," I said. "Still, there was this woman…"

"Yeah?" I could tell she was distracted. "Hold on a second." The television flared to full volume, and then was muffled as she apparently took control of the remote.

When she returned, I said, "I don't feel like there were any big insights."

"Well, you got at least one: 'The world is a big and beautiful place.' Isn't that what you texted me from Sacramento?"

"Oh, I didn't think that went through. Sure, it was a great trip in that way...but you don't get it. I'm a professor. There's an answer for every question if you just look hard enough and in the right places, but I have no answers. I don't feel like I'm over Paul in even the remotest way, but I did meet this woman on the train who told me she got to know her husband even better during his illness."

"But you had no clue Paul was going to die. Maybe he's trying to let you know him now. Hold on a second." She put the phone down as a child screamed. "Give me that remote back, right now. If you two can't watch this video in peace, you're both going to your rooms for the next hour. I'm trying to talk to Aunt Cheryl."

There was silence in the background as she returned to our conversation, warming to one of her favorite topics. "I mean, think of it, Cheryl. If you really love someone, why shouldn't that continue on after death? Who's to say he's not still trying to communicate with you? Remember that night I stayed at your house with you? You can't tell me all those sounds were normal. Mom and Dad noticed, too."

"Do you really think there's some kind of 'Paul ghost' haunting my house? All the more reason to sell the place. Now that Joe and his family have moved out, I don't need the space."

"Oh...I don't know, Cheryl. That might not be the best thing until you feel like you have closure with Paul's death. Maybe I should try the sage again. Did you burn those holy candles I bought?"

"Yes, every night. Hey, listen, we're coming up to a stop and I need to stretch my legs. I'll talk to you about this when I get back."

"We could do a séance. I've never done one before, but maybe that's what you need. I actually got some books at the New Age bookstore, and I'd be willing to try it."

"Beth, you know I don't believe in stuff like that." It was an ironic echo of the conversation we had shortly before I decided to take the trip.

"Well...just saying. I know Judy would come along."

Judy, a mutual friend, was even more into the psychic world than Beth; she had made a cast of her pregnant body in a celebrating motherhood ceremony one month before her due date.

Beth and a few other friends had been invited over, not knowing that Judy planned to disrobe and coat her body with plaster of Paris in front of them.

I hung up with a promise to "think about" Beth's suggestions and reached for the yellow pill that calmed me down whenever I got overly emotional. Then, as we cruised to a brief stop in Johnstown, I added, "Take fewer pills," to my list.

harrisburg, pa
the daily pennsylvanian

The Pennsylvania panorama outside my window flowed from trees to water to mountains to tiny towns and then stretches of familiar flat scrub against a backdrop of mountains. It felt like months had passed since Lee, the mystery train traveler, had sat next to me and we passed by the same geography. He was the first person I met on my trip, but he hadn't been the beginning of a process I had hoped would take place, i.e. a chain of wise individuals who would be my unique grief support group.

In graduate school, my studies of Freud, Carl Jung, Virginia Satir, and Carl Rogers helped me understand the importance of healthy connections with other people, but it was Dr. Irvin Yalom who intrigued me the most. Dr. Yalom believed that within the group setting, counseling and support can be even more powerful for many reasons: we can learn from and with others, try out new behaviors, and receive support as we process painful experiences. My dissertation studied the impact of support groups, and much of my work with girls and women is founded on the principle of connection with like-minded others in a safe environment to forge better relationships.

Shortly after Paul died I had attended a grief support group, believing there would be answers and solutions there for me, too. As I listened to the straightforward stories of others who shared their sadness in the opening introductions, it was clear I couldn't capture the traumatic events of my life so succinctly. "My daughter was in jail when my husband died. We had years of sorrow together about her problems." "I had to do CPR on him, but it didn't save him anyway." "We went to the hospital where I work and many of my coworkers showed up." "He was seriously drunk when he fell to his death." "I found out so many secrets about him after he died that I wondered if I even knew the real person he had been for our 28 years together."

Which story should I tell? I left the group feeling worse because I didn't have a simple story that could be shared in a sentence or two.

Esther made me realize that didn't matter. Having some time to "prepare" for her husband's death and even desiring that a loved one be relieved of suffering were part of the multifaceted process of grief, which could occur before or after a loved one died. We don't grieve more or less; we grieve differently.

After five years of caregiving, she had provided what we refer to as "quality of death"; it offered her peace after years of watching John decline, his pain increasing as time passed. They had smoothed out the bumps on the road of life, sorted through final memories, and even started planning for Esther's future alone. Maybe that was my problem; amidst the suddenness of Paul's fall and the rapid exposure of all his secrets, I hadn't had time to say goodbye—but I had discovered that it wasn't too late to do that.

For much of the time left in my trip, I thought about Esther. It was easy to feel sorry about her situation, since her husband hadn't put himself at risk for cancer, but Paul had engaged in behaviors that led to his illness. Although I didn't act on that idea just then, it began a train of thought that led me to educate myself about the nuances of alcoholism. After discovering that High Functioning Alcoholism. HFA was a real diagnosis in the psychiatric bible, the DSM, I did further research, discovering that those afflicted were often able to maintain demanding careers and relationships while consuming incredible quantities of alcohol. Often, HFA went unrecognized because they didn't conform to the stereotype of a vagabond with a bottle in a bag and were often smart enough to construct elaborate deceptions that covered up their behavior.

Thinking that Paul had a diagnosable medical problem would shift something deeper inside me that had begun when I first compared my grief with Esther's. Alcohol had been part of our relationship from the beginning, a seductive lover who could beckon him into a private world where he wasn't anxious or sad. It had a power over him greater me or his children's.

It would never be possible to know how hard he tried to stop. Our joint therapist told me he had cried several times right before his death, admitting things were so bad he couldn't go on, but his secretary, Sue, who saw him every work day for years, was quite definite about his continued drinking.

Fortunately, I had a double seat to myself at that point, because as we neared Harrisburg, I cried, but not the harsh sobs of fury and grief from the early months of bereavement and not the reluctant tears that came thereafter when a tug of war between sorrow and anger plagued me. My grief was slow, with the kind of tears that welled up until they spilled over.

It was okay to feel sad and mad, along with a blender of other emotions each time I pushed the buttons of the past. Being angry with Paul didn't diminish mourning over his absence, or my regret for the tormented life he lived, but now there was a relief in knowing that the pain of his existence had ended.

That was Esther's gift. She, too, had raged over her husband's illness when it was first diagnosed, but she had made it external to him and a mutual enemy they faced together. I hadn't been Paul's partner in battling his addictions to the degree I could have, but maybe I had given him a stable social structure that prevented it from becoming worse.

If only he could have held on to that one time Mark referred to when we paddled around the little lake in the boat, blissfully happy after reconciling. Maybe that could have launched a move away from alcohol and pills and toward a healthy lifestyle. For at least a year after that day, we swam together regularly, ate good food, and remembered what made us fall in love. He smiled a lot and seemed genuinely happy, but then gradually, he withdrew again. At the time, I took it as a sign he didn't love me, but as the train rocked its way back to Harrisburg, I realized that he had most likely been lured back to alcohol.

I could never again tell students or patients and their families and friends—that grief ended, although I desperately wanted to believe that it did. Nor would I believe in a guarantee that life would eventually reach a stage of "not unhappy," but I had been given an epiphany on the trip. I was beginning to accept Paul for who he truly was and how he truly lived, even if it had painful repercussions.

As the conductor announced our pending arrival at the Harrisburg train station, I gathered up my belongings, thinking that maybe tiny doses of those things could gain momentum and I could charge forward into the future, as swiftly and certainly as the train that just taken me across the country and back.

The airbrakes screeched, and we hissed to a stop. The conductor's voice boomed over the PA system.

"Ladies and gentlemen, for your safety, please take care when transitioning from the train to the platform."

With an empty book of tickets and new Hello Kitty suitcase, I surely intended to try.

hershey, pa

When I stepped off the train in Harrisburg and back into my "regular" life in Hershey, was there a mythical bridge between past to present that I hoped for? At the time, I thought not because my second year of widowhood was just as challenging as the first, partly because most of the people I knew were like me. They thought the hard work of grieving would be finished in twelve months and I would be back to baseline Cheryl: multitasking, mothering, working, writing, and swimming...but not wife-ing. Instead, I was post-crisis Cheryl, shocked by what had happened in the previous year, half convinced another tsunami of grief was about to bowl me over, and alone but for Granddear and Lacey.

No one wanted to hear that my circumstances were "extraordinary," even if they were. My feeble explanations ("We never got to say goodbye, so there's no sense of closure," or "Doing CPR on your husband is something you can never get over") just didn't cut it anymore, even if they sounded pretty impressive to me. Even I got tired of hearing the words but couldn't stop myself from sharing them over and over.

Following up on my sister's suggestion to consult with a clairvoyant began to seem like a good idea. I wanted the kind of finality Esther had, a "The End" to the story of Paul and Me, and if it meant allowing a stranger to reach into the Great Beyond, so be it.

Although what happened in the session countered every scientific principle I believed in, the woman I sought out knew shockingly specific details of my life. I had only given her my first name and blocked my phone number so she couldn't track any information about me, but as soon as she settled into the moment of reaching out to Paul, she asked about his mother (by name) and told me my son's ear troubles were something that needed serious attention. Then my clairvoyant invited me to ask any questions of my husband that I wanted.

"Are you in heaven?" was the first one.

"He says he is in a place where he had to go to 'learn some things,'" she answered.

"Are you okay?" was the next.

"He's okay," she said.

We continued our exchange this way, with me asking a multitude of questions, including what Paul thought would happen with our daughter.

"He says he thinks she's trying really hard to do better."

There was a bit of silence as I pondered the most important question I had come with. Finally, taking a deep breath, I asked, "Were you drunk when you fell?"

It was an eerie moment—the lights actually flickered and for a moment the noisy basement air conditioner near where we were sitting went still. The clairvoyant, who was holding both of my hands in hers, wasn't so much shocked as curious.

"He's gone," she told me. "I've never had this happen before." Then, a few seconds later she announced he was back, and had communicated the answer to my question: "Yes."

My body seemed to turn to air even though part of me was ready to express my disbelief. Before I could say anything, she shared a long message from Paul, assuring me that I was a good mother and had done all the right things for our children.

The session, which I taped, lasted about an hour, and although the idea of a total stranger offering so many insights to my life disturbed me, my wish had been fulfilled: I got answers to the many questions that had continued to twist and turn in my brain since Paul died. That felt like the beginning of closure. On the way out, I paid the clairvoyant the same amount as my copayment for "real" therapy.

Was it genuine? When I listened to the recording again, it was impossible to deny that something unusual had happened. Again and again, I tried to rationalize how the woman I had never met and knew of only through a friend of a friend, could have hit the mark on so many of my questions, or staged a mini blackout in her basement.

"Of course it was true," my sister said when I shared the story with her. "The Bible talks about people who have the gift of communicating with the dead—why don't you believe it?" Neither of us knew then that in another year, she would have a vivid dream about Paul where he informed her he was in a "good place" and encouraged her to tell me all was well.

It was also a surprise when Jack floated back into my life several months after my train trip, claiming to still have "feelings" for me and insisting the loss of our relationship threw him into a serious depression. By then, I was interested in another person, but some of his old charm convinced me to meet him for a drink where we dissected the good, bad, and downright ugly of our past in the same way families rehash shared memories during holiday meals. It didn't convince me to give him a second chance, but that didn't stop him from trying a third and fourth time.

After reading an earlier draft of this memoir, Jack even "borrowed" my train trip theme and self-published a book of his own about life choices, which I realized was his classic behavior, complimenting and punishing me in one gesture. At least I was healthy enough by then to recognize it for what it was.

"You saved my life and then ripped my heart apart," I told him during one of his final attempts to reconcile.

Turning Jack down didn't diminish my longing for a steady partner. In the years of my marriage, it seemed the world had somehow become coupled—wherever I went, people were in pairs. Going to the movies and eating out alone had never been a problem for me when Paul was alive but being forced to do so after he died made the experience uncomfortable.

In my second year of widowhood, I did begin to accept my new life and to heal. Beth and I continued to talk about the books we could/would write, and I suddenly had more time to spend with my parents, who began to look aged. Granddear, of course, could always make me smile, and I was fortunate to be able to spend at least one afternoon every week with her.

I accepted that we can never understand death completely but must rely on the presence of whatever is positive and good in our lives to help us survive the ride on the grief train that will inevitably come. I had taken a journey that gave me time to regroup in a new but temporary environment and came back to where I started from different, if not beginning to be better.

And Paul? If I embraced the unknowable, it meant believing that he had taken a journey into strange territory, too, and hopefully a dream my sister had about him smiling and happy was right, and things turned out well. On the second anniversary of his death, he was finally buried with the big headstone bearing both of our names that he wanted. Sometimes, I would lie in the grass before it as if he was next to me and look up at the bottle blue cloudless sky of summer, talking as if he was next to me.

"I still miss you," or "Help me figure out what to do next," or "You'll always be my OAO." (OAO was a term from his college days when his fraternity brothers used to describe their "One and Only" girlfriends back home.)

If I were in the same classroom today teaching Death and Dying to young people, I would tell them that each person is unique and that I can only attest to what I have learned not from books or experts but my own experience. The rough journey of my grief returned me to where I started as a different person, awed by the bigness of this world and the degree of pain some suffer but manage to prevail.

Maybe I would encourage students to take a trip that forces them to be totally alone in the midst of people or perhaps I might suggest they listen to as many stories of loss as they could endure. Finally, I might end our class with the Jewish Mourner's Kaddish, a blessing that offered me so much comfort in the days immediately after my husband died.

Blessed and praised, glorified and exalted, extolled and honored, elevated and lauded be the Name of the Holy One, blessed be He, (blessed be He) beyond all the blessings and hymns, praises and consolations that are spoken in the world; and say, Amen.

And so I say, Amen.

epilogue

It's been over a decade since Paul died and my life has continued to change, leading me to believe my years with him were the most stable ones I will ever experience—but if Mark is right, and I live to 86, there I still plenty of time left to test out that theory. I continue to take the train as often as possible, sometimes with Granddear, who is now a teenager, and sometimes by myself on the way to an adventure. When I met a man who lived an hour away but on the train route, I regularly grabbed the 5 p.m. commuter headed east toward Philadelphia and savored the ride to be with him, enjoying the anticipation of the weekend with my fellow travelers.

I married that man after two years of dating and gained some lovely additions to my family that still continue, but much of our relationship fractured and fell apart the longer we spent together. When I consulted a therapist three years after our wedding (and very close to the 6th anniversary of Paul's death), she listened to a description of the new husband's behavior and gave me a book to read on narcissism, declaring him "a textbook case." After being forced by another therapist to admit he had deceived me in ways the counselor described as "unforgivable," our divorce was more acrimonious than the crushing split with Jack. It's not surprising that I have now sworn off any future marriages, but I do continue to date and have met some good men who haven't caused trauma.

My conversation with Paul the night before he died made me sad for the many goals he would never achieve, but it also inspired me not to delay opportunities. One thing I regretted but supposed would never happen was completing my MFA in creative writing. It was the degree I wanted to pursue after I graduated from high school, but my parents thought nursing was more likely to get me a job—or find me wedded to a doctor. Although I substituted writing conferences, workshops, and periodic college courses for the education I really wanted, when I attended a summer writing retreat that made me decide it wasn't too late, I applied to a program within commuting distance and was accepted as a part-time student.

The program was everything I had dreamed of in my teenaged years, secluded in my bedroom with a pen and notebook, crafting a romance novel that I felt sure would be the first of many. In my MFA program, I renewed my interest in poetry, friendships, and fun, but it was an event that took place during my first semester that felt like Paul was cheering me on.

In a workshop where we critiqued each other's creative nonfiction writing, one student shared the story of her father's "secret" drinking problem. As I listened to her read about his hidden bottles, I knew she was describing the diagnosis of "High Functioning Alcoholic (HFA)." If seeing the clairvoyant provided some kind of ending to the story of Paul's death, educating myself about HFA and hearing her story wiped away the remnants of my guilt. In its place, I wondered, *What had been the "real Paul" and the "HFA Paul"*? The answer to that question wasn't easy since it wasn't until my husband died that I really knew him.

As I completed my coursework and prepared to write my thesis, I thought about using a novel I had come very close to publishing. It would be a chance to refine it so my agent could try and sell it, but of course, I rarely choose the easy options in life.

Instead, I looked through the messy pages I had started about my trip and decided it was an opportunity to write an important story that might help me personally. Putting together the narrative of my most significant life event was the hardest writing I've done. At times, I cried over a particularly painful memory. At others, I couldn't open the file containing the manuscript to write anymore. Had it not been for my advisor, who moved me along with several suggestions that changed the book for the better, I may have given up. Once finished and shared with others, it added to my understanding and acceptance of what happened.

The peace I now feel over what happened began to fit together like pieces of a jigsaw puzzle. My children are all thriving, and I continue to teach compassionate and intelligent medical students. For over two decades, I have worked as a volunteer within the penal system, counseling women of all ages who were adjudicated, incarcerated, in work-release, or post-release—and that has helped as well. When she was younger, my daughter would come with me at times, helping to entertain young children who were visiting their mothers. Then, as I progressed to facilitating a writing group, an older woman who would become my "prison mentor" shared her wisdom about connecting with others who may have been educated and lived lives differently.

On a few occasions, I have shared a bit of my own writing with the women—once, a poem about my daughter being ill and incarcerated, which they thought I had made up. Another time, when I handed out an essay about "the grief train," it surprised them to find out I had experienced the kind of emotional pain so common to them.

I still miss Paul. I miss him in the role of grandfather to our six granddaughters and I miss him sharing tidbits of information with me about history, mystery books he had read, or interesting events from his work. I miss his presence, which may have been subdued at times but was always there. We all miss him when my children and I celebrate holidays together, especially Christmas when my youngest son has taken to wearing the plaid vest passed down from Joe Senior to Paul and now him.

Yes he is still with me, in an easier way than before, mostly in my heart and mind. He's a bit bittersweet but a part of my life I will always hold on to because the gift of our years together comforts me, even though our real time relationship has ended.

Paul and I went on two separate journeys. Mine was a rough trip cushioned by a lullaby that made it all bearable. I can't know what his travels have been like, but I believe that someday, I will find out.

about the author

Cheryl Dellasega is a nurse practitioner with a PhD in health education and counseling along with a "bucket list" MFA, which she finished in 2015. Her academic work has generated hundreds of scholarly presentations and publications on caregiving and female relationships at international venues along with a visiting professorship in Sweden. Currently, she teaches medical students at the Penn State College of Medicine, is a nurse consultant for research at Penn State Health, and is the founder of Club and Camp Ophelia. As an award-winning author, she has written five books on female relationships *(Surviving Ophelia, Girl Wars, The Starving Family, Mean Girls Grow Up,* and *Forced to be Family)*, a fiction series for girls *(blggrls)*, and two nursing books *(What to do When Nurses Hurt Nurses* and *Toxic Nursing)*.

www.ingramcontent.com/pod-product-compliance
Lightning Source LLC
Chambersburg PA
CBHW050856150626
46549CB00013B/2337